The ESSENTIAL HUMILITY *of* MARRIAGE

The ESSENTIAL HUMILITY *of* MARRIAGE

Honoring the Third Identity
in Couple Therapy

Terry D. Hargrave, Ph.D.

ZEIG, TUCKER & THEISEN, INC.
PHOENIX, ARIZONA

Library of Congress Cataloging-in-Publication Data

Hargrave, Terry D.
    The essential humility of marriage : honoring the third identity in couple therapy / Terry D. Hargrave.
        p.   cm.
    Includes bibliographical references and index.
    ISBN1-891944-36-3
    1. Marital psychotherapy.   2. Family psychotherapy.
    3. Interpersonal relations.   I. Title.

RC488.5.H3549 2000
616.89'156—dc21

                                                00-025245

Published by
Zeig, Tucker & Theisen, Inc.
3618 North 24th Street
Phoenix, AZ 85016

Book design by Kathleen Lake, Neuwirth & Associates, Inc.

Manufactured in the United States of America

10   9   8   7   6   5   4   3   2   1

stability
security
sincerity

To the "Us" that is
between Sharon and Terry

Contents

Preface

Three couples come to mind when I think about this book on marriage. The first involves partners who had previous marriages, both caught up in the initial intoxication of interest, erotic love, and nurture that leads from a deep attraction to possible enduring companionship. They are just on the threshold of making something great. Then there is a couple that has been married 19 years. This is their first marriage and they have two children; both also have demanding schedules. They love each other deeply, but they find their intimacy suffers in the mad rush to get everything done when there are too many demands and not enough resources. The third couple has been married for 62 years. Their children and their children's children have long since grown up. They still nurture each other and are so much a part of one another that it is difficult to tell where one begins and the other leaves off.

There is an essential quality that these three couples share. The common quality is one of "us-ness." By this I mean that these couples have bound themselves together in a relationship that creates a third entity, an entity that exists between two individuals. "Us" is not quite one or the other, but has elements of both individuals. "Us" is that place that holds the love and trust and what the two people have together. "Us" is invisible, but it is real, kept alive by each partner's nurturing, loving, and trustworthy contributions.

This book is about the marital "us." As a therapist, I know that when marriages are good, like the ones mentioned above, they can be very good. But when marriages are bad, they can be very bad indeed. I have come to believe that it is how the partners have treated their relational "us" that has the greatest impact on whether or not the marriage is good or bad.

As a therapist, I have learned that working with couples in this area requires moving them toward making some adjustments in attitude before introducing techniques. For techniques to take root, partners must have recommitted themselves to the "us" of their relationship.

This commitment is built on three essential ingredients: stability, security, and sincerity. I try to demonstrate how therapy can assist couples to acknowledge the resources that already exist, and to develop greater strengths where necessary so they can live together without fear of harm, do the daily work of marriage in a trustworthy way, and learn to grow as individuals and in relationship.

I have not tried to detail every situation or problem that couples present in therapy. I believe that the attitudes I discuss are applicable to myriad situations and problems, but there are many issues that are not specifically addressed in these pages. Keep in mind that most of my case examples represent married relationships. Although it is true that some 4.1 million people live with their partners outside of marriage, and I believe that most of the principles outlined here are applicable, I still find that most enduring relationships are in marriages or end up in marriages. Finally, this book is about clinical work, and not research. It is a practical guide for therapists who need help and direction in assisting couples to a better relationship.

—Terry D. Hargrave

Acknowledgments

I am grateful to many who have helped me produce this work. First, to my friend, Malcolm Street. Without his faithful support and encouragement, I would never have had the precious gift of time to write. Second, to the many couples that I have seen in therapy. They are continued inspiration. Third, to the three couples I described in the preface. They have given me more living material on marriage than anyone could ever find in the endless stacks of books on the shelves. Finally, to my wife, Sharon. She is truly my soul mate who helps makes "us" more stable, secure, and sincere. She has made my life complete. She has made my life peaceful. She has made my life fun.

—Terry D. Hargrave

Section I

The Promise of "Us"

chapter one

What Makes Relationships Work

Most couples have no idea why they divorce. They may have reasons: an unfaithful spouse, abuse, or feeling unfulfilled and unhappy. But most couples are totally unaware of how their marriages slowly fell apart to be eventually destroyed by irresponsible and destructive actions. Obviously, they do not start out intending to divorce. They marry full of hope and deeply in love with each other. They are willing to make sacrifices, happy to pledge lifelong loyalty for the financial, social, emotional, and spiritual good of the other. Such commitments are usually witnessed by family and friends, as these couples fully expect to go the distance together.

By the time couples come to our offices, circumstances have usually deteriorated so much that they hurl insult after insult at each other, engaging in character assassinations and sealing themselves off emotionally so that they are rarely touched by any tender feelings from the relationship. They now invest their emotional energies, once reserved for their spouses, in their work, families of origin, children, friends, or lovers. They may lie to each other to avoid confrontation or to create distance. These couples are as far apart as they can get while still being together.

How did this downward spiral begin? Couples have difficulty identifying what went wrong. And the fact is, most professionals who do marriage therapy have the same difficulty. It is not because we are not smart enough. Most of us have been trained to spot dysfunctional patterns and poor communication. We apply what we know with empathy and vigor. We even find that our efforts are helpful to some couples. But often our therapies are too little, too late. We teach techniques. We coach people on how to avoid old patterns. And, in the end, we miss the heart of what is wrong with the relationship. Our techniques help with the symptoms, but they do not always address the core issues. Therefore, treatments meet with limited success and have a tendency to become less effective over time. As professional marriage therapists, we need to be able to correctly identify what goes wrong in these relationships so that we can help couples to find their way back to a nurturing and secure marital connection.

This book is about intervening with couples in a way that gets to the heart of the problem. It is a clinical book that draws on 14 years of doing marital therapy, and it is designed to help therapists ferret out with their clients the essential attitudes that keep a marriage alive and to reveal the key issues that undermine the relationship. The premise is that a couple's ability to learn marital techniques and use them effectively over the long term is directly related to the ability to create profound attitudinal shifts in the relationship—to move from resignation to destination.

What Goes Wrong

I have been married for twenty years and have known my wife since we were in the eighth grade. My wife and I have a strong, happy marriage. Many of my students ask me, "What makes your marriage happy?" I must confess that for years I would answer, "I don't know." I knew that I had a good marriage, but I did not know what the essential quality was that made it so. Was it that my wife made me happy? Was it that the relationship fulfilled me personally? Was it because we had good communication and intimacy? Yes, yes, and yes—sometimes. Other times, things did not run so smoothly, and yet the relationship seemed to keep working.

So, what is the ingredient that makes my marriage successful? At first, my thinking was that couples in struggling marriages had simply stopped trying. These couples likely vowed to walk hand in hand on their journey through life, but instead of a straight, flat road, they found the trail of marriage leading into a maze. Every turn they took would potentially lead them into a more confusing and difficult spot. Confusion led to more frustration, and, inevitably, the partners turned on one another and started jockeying for the more powerful position to make the decisions that would lead them out of the maze. Blaming ensued as each would accuse the other of making the wrong decision or of not being cooperative enough. Sooner or later, the couple would invent individual strategies to deal with the confusion and frustration, strategies that excluded the partner. They parted company in the maze, hoping they would meet up in a better place. But as each partner moved on his or her own course, they moved further and further apart from the marriage. I believed for many years that it was that the partners had just lost each other. It was the confusion and frustration, the power struggles and the blaming, that were the problem. So, like many therapists, I worked on the communication and pattern strategies with couples to interrupt the downward spiral of frustration and blaming and the therapy met with only limited success.

When I saw how difficult it was for couples to change these destructive patterns, I began to do a little blaming myself. I came to see the couples that were seeking my help as being unwilling to make the commitment necessary to do the hard work of learning the skills of communication. Why were they unwilling? In my mind, it was because they did not have a clue about how to "do" a relationship. The fault lay, at least in part, with a couple's expectation of marriage. I felt that most couples came to marriage with the idea that they would carry out the activities of marriage. To these couples, marriage was a contract whereby they would work to provide goods and services to each other—bearing children, achieving financial goals, having friends, fulfilling community obligations. So the fault lay, I believed, in the couple's lack of understanding concerning the real work of marriage. Marriage was about intimacy and growing together. I defined intimacy as the ability to share thoughts, feelings, or emotions with your spouse. In return, your spouse understood you, but you also came to understand yourself better. When couples would not follow my directives and use the communication techniques I provided in therapy, I assumed that they were unwilling to give up the "goods and services" definition of marriage and see the true meaning of marriage.

Even with these conclusions in place, I had the nagging feeling that I was not quite getting to the heart of the problem. If couples did not know the real reasons behind their divorces and I could not pinpoint why a marriage was strong, the essential elements in building healthy relationships were at best vague and at worst missing entirely. All the rules, techniques, and good intentions in the world would not build a strong couple relationship.

The Promise of "Us"

There were some truths in what I had believed about the problems I saw in the failing relationships that came to me, but they were not quite the whole story. Couples had, for the most part, started out their lives together well meaning and hopeful, and then became trapped in the confusion and disappointment. What I began to realize was that these couples had not just lost one another, they had lost their relationship.

This concept of the relationship as an entity separate from but dependent on the partners is difficult to understand, and yet it is essential. It is not just that two individuals participate together in an exchange for each other's good, it is that they create a whole new being when they marry. I was first introduced to this concept by the pioneering family therapist, Carl Whitaker. One time during a conversation over breakfast, he was talking about his wife. Carl said that as much as he would miss her if she were to die, he would miss what they were together even more. He would call what they were together "we-ness" or "us-ness." What is exciting about this concept of "us-ness" is that it is not quite me, and not quite you. "Us" is what we are together. "Us" is created by two individuals in a committed relationship; it takes on a personality with characteristics of its own. It is not just two individuals who share, it is two individuals who give up part of themselves to create a oneness, an "us." This is not "the two shall become one" as much as it is the two shall become three. There's my wife and I, and there's "us," which has its own personality, its own likes and dislikes. For instance, I don't like ballet, but "us" does. When I say this, I do not mean that I do not like ballet and I just give in to my wife because she likes it and I suffer through a performance. I mean that when I go with my wife, the activity becomes enjoyable because of how we dress up to go, where we go to eat, and how we interact about the performance. Our relationship really does like the activity of ballet, even though I would never go by myself. But it is not only in the activities of "us," it also has personality characteristics that are predictable. I can tell when "us" is getting ready to have a fight. "Us" may be invisible, but it is a living and breathing relationship that is kept alive by my wife and me being engaged in trustworthy giving.

"Us-ness" is the relationship. It transcends each person in the relationship, but depends on the individuals to keep it alive. It is the "us" that is the essential element in keeping marriage together, because, in fact, it is the only part of the spouses that is together. In family therapy theory, we are taught a useful concept of individuation (Bowen, 1978). Essential in this concept of individuation is the ability of a person to balance the drive for his or her individuality with the drive to be in a relationship. Balance between individuality and relationship, or individuation, means that a person is able to be in a relationship and at the same time is secure in knowing who he or she is as an individual.

In most Western societies, we have overfocused on individuality for the last 40 to 50 years. In psychology in particular, the focus in the therapeutic world has been on individual self-esteem movements, asserting individual rights, expressing feelings, and achieving personal satisfaction and happiness. These ideas have permeated our culture so thoroughly that we seldom even think to challenge the logic. As a society, we have come to believe that most disturbing things that individuals do are the result of damaged self-esteem; if individuals find societal roadblocks in the way of self-actualization, they need to be more assertive in achieving their goals; if people feel something, they have a right and a psychological need to express the feeling no matter what the emotional fallout may be; and most important, if individuals are not happy, they should be able to change their situations or relationships to make themselves happier. Individuals *deserve* to be happy and satisfied.

I can speculate that this overfocus on individuality is most likely the result of decades and centuries of people having to sacrifice their individual needs and desires to the needs and desires of others. In modern history, it is not difficult to find social classes or social institutions that were more than willing to deny the needs and wants of individuals in order to fulfill that particular entity's goals and desires.

Since antiquity until the 17th century, it was the church that defined marriage as an institution designed exclusively for the purpose of procreation and service to God (Saxton, 1993). And it was the abuses of leadership in the church and the misuse of power that undoubtedly laid the foundations for patriarchy and helped to foster today's bigotry and racism. After the 17th century, the civil government was the institution that governed marriage. Through laws and dictates, the government set various restrictions on what roles and practices individuals could pursue (Saxton, 1993). For example, many governments specified laws to restrict marriage to one between one man and one woman. This ensured that children from the marriage would be the legitimate heirs to the marriage estate and avoid disruption in the transfer of money and property. Social stability was the goal of the civil government, often to the advantage of one group at the expense of another.

For instance, during the first half of this century, the men in the family were able to exploit the women and to restrict them to traditional, less important roles by exercising their superior strength and social power. Patriarchy, of course, still survives today, but women in Western society have made significant strides toward satisfying their needs and desires as individuals. The point is that before the humanistic movement of the last 40 to 50 years, a person's self-worth could be made subservient to the wants of a more powerful person or group. Thus, to be in a relationship meant that one risked losing one's selfhood in deference to control by someone or something else.

What does this have to do with "us-ness?" It is difficult to find evidence that we have ever had a true concept of the "us" relationships being a vital part of the marriage. For centuries, relationships have demanded personal sacrifice to the point that little or no individuality remains. the focus on individuality for the last 50 years has recognized the importance of individual goals, dreams, and satisfaction, with satisfying relationships viewed as simply a way to gain further individual happiness. The options have traditionally been limited: you either are yourself as an individual and alone or you compromise or deny your individuality in order to maintain a relationship with another.

The heart of "us" is not that I sacrifice my individuality for my wife, but that I willingly give a part of who I am for the sake of the relationship. When I give, and my wife gives, we bond parts of ourselves together to create a unique new entity called "us." It is the mutual giving to the relationship that, in turn, creates the context for intimacy found in the relationship of "us." In this way, sex often provides a good picture of intimacy. Sexual activity at its best means that I focus on satisfying my wife. And as a result of the way that I am made, the very thing that I give to her ends up bringing me satisfaction that culminates in orgasm. Now I think that orgasm is a good thing. But one aspect that makes it really interesting is that once orgasm begins, it becomes a series of involuntary contractions that dump all that built-up sexual energy. Think about it. Sex is one of the few activities in which we consciously lose control of ourselves with another person. This is truly a golden highway—I give to my beloved in such a complete way that I lose part of myself in the process. And it is not a painful loss, but a loss that culminates in a blissful "ahhh."

The ability to be out of control physically, emotionally naked, and yet totally at peace in the presence of another person, this is what this trustworthy giving yields, whether in physical sex or emotional intimacy. We give of ourselves to bind ourselves with a spouse in an "us" relationship, but creating an "us" does not mean that we lose ourselves. The "us" becomes a nurturer to our individuality that works both to teach us and to fulfill our personal desires. This is one of life's paradoxes, that as we give up part of our individuality to create this "us" relationship, we gain nurturance for our own personhood. When we give to "us," we actually receive.

What is the result of this losing of myself in the sexual experience if my wife and I aren't using a birth-control technique and the planets are aligned right? Conception, of course. Half of my genetic material meets half of hers to create a new human being. I like to think of my children as testimonies to the struggle in which my wife and I engage in order to be intimate. They are different from me and from their mother, and they are physical representations of our invisible "us-ness."

This "us" is what marriage is. The real heart of what makes a marriage satisfying and happy is a strong and vital "us." It is not how the partners communicate or how often they encounter, and overcome, obstacles. Most couples have difficulty with communicating and have to face hard realities in life. It is the quality of "us" that either allows the spouses to hang together and hold each other close through good times and bad, or forces them to take destructive actions in the name of self-preservation. Couples have strong marriages because they have learned how to sacrifice for the good of the "us" relationship and how to utilize the relationship to encourage their goals and fulfill their needs as individuals. In good marriages, persons truly balance the ability to maintain individuality and to serve the relationship. Couples have weak and struggling marriages because one partner or both see individual needs as preeminent. The idea of sacrifice for the sake of "us" is either ignored or nonexistent and partners are forced into a position of competing for self-fulfillment. The sense of relationship together becomes weakened and begins to disappear as the individual ego or egos become the predominant force. In these competitive marriages, couples not only lose each other, they lose the relationship. When "us" is lost, the actions that individuals will take in order to feel "fulfilled" can be extremely destructive—including infidelity, violence, stealing, manipulation, and substance abuse.

What Marriage Is, What It Is Not

If marriage is this "us" relationship, why are couples so resistant or so hesitant to do things that will nurture the relationship and help it thrive. There is no doubt that part of the problem is the obsession with individualism that our society has supported. However, another significant component is that couples have no language or overt support for the idea of giving to the "us" relationship. Because "us" is invisible, it is easy to neglect. Because "us" is hard to define, it has been left undefined and unidentified for most couples. The part of marriage that can be seen—contractual obligations and activities—is the part the couples attends to in one way or another. Ask most people what marriage is and they will give you some explanation involving legal arrangements, and then move quickly to a description of the activities that surround marriage. Indeed, marriage is a contract that has a variety of legal implications, and it is infused with all sorts of activities, from the mundane to the profound, but these descriptions are like looking at a map and mistaking it for the actual land.

Maps are useful in gaining perspective, but they are not the soil of the real territory. The territory in marriage is the "us" relationship—the map highlights the contractual obligations and activities. In order to bring about hopeful changes in relationships, therapy cannot be focussed on making modification to the maps; it must concentrate on helping and educating the couple about the relationship itself.

The Purpose of Marriage

Why do I need this "us" relationship? What useful purpose does it serve? Some would say that the purpose of marriage is to provide intimacy and a sense of belonging. Although most people would acknowledge that humans are compelled by a variety of drives to seek intimacy, many models, such as attachment and humanistic theories (i.e., Maslow, 1971; Dreikurs & Soltz, 1964; Ainsworth, 1989), maintain that intimacy and belonging are basic human needs that must be fulfilled to arouse healthy individuality.

The question becomes: Is intimacy an end in and of itself? Most definitions of intimacy center on ideas of closeness, warmth, trust, affection, and self-disclosure (Perlman & Duck, 1987). I would argue that intimacy does include these concepts, but that the definition should not be limited to types of descriptors that make it sound as if intimacy is simply a means to fulfill the desires of the individual. Intimacy is a basic human need, not because it satisfies our desires, but because self-awareness and other-awareness are fostered by it.

The ideas of Martin Buber (1958) are relevant here. Buber maintained that there is a relational imperative built into existence. Relationships function as mirrors of our individual selves, and as we interact with others, the relationship tells us about ourselves. Intimacy becomes then more than satisfaction, it becomes revelation. Buber, thus, believed that if I am going to understand myself as *I*, I must be in a relationship with you or *thou*. It is in this mix of the *I* and *thou* that I can know myself and become self-aware.

The whole point of intimacy in any relationship is to know yourself. It is by relationship that your true self is revealed in such a way that you can see and understand it. Once you understand, you can grow into deeper levels of relationship and self-understanding. So intimacy is not an end itself, but a means of achieving individual understanding and growth. Kieffer (1977) has perhaps captured this idea best, defining intimacy as being the experiencing of the essence of one's self in physical, intellectual, and emotional communication with another.

It is easy to see how relationships with a child are not designed simply to meet the child's needs, but are intended to meet those needs so that he or she can grow physically, intellectually, and emotionally. But when those children grow up, somehow we no longer see them as dependent on relationships to help them to continue to grow as adults.

I believe that the purpose of marriage, like any relationship in life, is to help us mature and become fulfilled as an individual. In short, the purpose of marriage is to grow us up!

Keeping "Us" Alive

Broadly speaking, "us" is kept alive by the two essential qualities in all relationships: love and trust. The essentials, then, are no less important in a marital relationship and we bank on them as we learn to be intimate with our spouses. Love is an idea that gets a lot of press in marriage therapy and other places. It is the primary reason most people give for getting married.

Love

There are different ways to conceptualize love, but it is difficult to define. One way to discuss love is to put it in the context of *feelings*. These feelings can range from connectedness or warmth to passion and sexual excitement. We can describe this kind of love as erotic or romantic love (Grunebaum, 1997). This type of love is characterized by longing and a strong desire to be physically and emotionally intimate. The beloved is idealized and is constantly in one's thoughts. It is similar in definition to the Greek *eros*, which means self-satisfying or erotic love.

Another way to think about love is in the context of *interactions* through which satisfying relationships are built on gratifying activities that meet the needs of companionship, trust, and tolerance. We can describe this type of love as companionate love (Saxton, 1993). The main idea here is that love takes on the essential elements of friendship, including enjoyment, mutual assistance, respect, acceptance, understanding, and admiration. This concept of love is similar to that described by the Greek term *phileo*, which is the love of one who has similar goals and emotions.

Finally, we can talk about love in the context of *giving* or *sacrifice*. In this type of love, people give up what they want or need for the good or need of the beloved. We can describe this type of love as being altruistic love (Saxton, 1993). The primary idea in altruistic love is that the giver actually receives satisfaction from the activity of meeting the needs of the receiver. The Greek term *agape* is very closely allied with this idea of altruism, which essentially means giving at the expense of one's self.

When we speak of marital love, which one do we mean? All of them, of course, but degrees of love will vary in any particular context. For instance, the degree of altruistic love one feels for a child may exceed that which he or she feels for the spouse. Much of the degree of love depends on the needs of the relationship and the individual personalities of the people involved. And although there are varying degrees of love in each context, all three types are necessary in a marital relationship. Each type of love communicates something essential to our being as an individual.

When we engage in family relationships, we essentially make ourselves dependent on those relationships to tell us *who we are* as individuals and *how we should act* in going about life. How we are loved gives us the information That describes *who we are* as people. And a marital relationship is unique in its ability to give us such information because it is a relationship that we choose. We stand with a person and we become a family by virtue of our pledges to love and honor each other. Because this relationship comes about by choice and not by biology, it affords perhaps the most dramatic opportunity for the demonstration of love and trust.

Erotic/Romantic Love

This type of love is wonderful in that it tells us that we are *unique* and *precious*. When someone looks at us with adoration, seems fascinated by whatever we say and do, wants to do everything possible to be in our presence, we cannot help but feel special. Nothing raises our self-esteem so much as being put on a pedestal and adored. When we see ourselves through the eyes of someone who loves us with this erotic/romantic love, we become a person without flaws, or at least with flaws that do not matter. We seldom feel this way specifically about ourselves, even though we have a profound need to do so. Erotic/romantic love meets that need by confirming that there is nobody quite like us and that we are appreciated beyond compare. All of us need to be loved in this way, especially by our spouses.

It has been suggested that people have little control over feeling this type of love and that, although it is relatively rare, it is essential to marital happiness (Grunebaum, 1997). Clinical experience will tell you that for most couples who have been married for any length of time, erotic/romantic love diminishes over the course of their marriage. These factors are difficult to reconcile when we talk about our need for erotic/romantic love from a spouse. If we cannot control the feeling that we consider essential to marital happiness, but it is usual for that feeling to decrease in correlation with the years that we are married, where is the hope for our continuing to have our need for this type of love met?

Clearly, it is extremely important that we see all types of love in terms of degree along a continuum rather than as on/off switches. The high end of the erotic/romantic love continuum would include those factors of intense sexual attraction, fascination, and a sense of mystery, similar to those feelings of first love back in high school. But even the low end of erotic/romantic love has essential elements of regard, admiration, and desire. This type of love may wax and wane in intensity throughout a marriage, but if the "us" relationship is alive, it seldom really dies. Our need to be the object of erotic/romantic love also may wax and wane, but we never totally lose our need to be loved in this way.

Companionate Love

There are so many things in life that are difficult. When you think about it, we are never in control of much of anything. Our physical life or health can be taken from us just as quickly as an accident can happen, our houses and other hard-earned material goods can be swept away in the short time it takes for a natural disaster to occur, and our financial success is always one day away from ruin. How do we make it when reality can be so hard?

Companionate love meets our need to know that *we are not alone*. When we have companionate love, we have a companion who likes us and who knows that we will walk through life together in good times and bad. Our companion enjoys our being and is comfortable when we are around. This person can trust us to be a listening ear and give assistance when it is needed. If terrible things happen, we will understand and be there. And our companion will do the same for us. Companionate love assures us that we are not alone.

It is essential that marital love include companionate love. When we choose a spouse, the quality of the friendship and companionship is perhaps the most important predictor of marital success (Rubin, 1985). To have a spouse who loves us in this way means having a good and true friend, and one whose life is parallel to our own because of the children, activities, family and assets we share.

Altruistic Love

When someone gives to us in a sacrificial way, it tells us that *we are worthy*. When I think about altruistic love, I think about true sacrifice. A dramatic example is in the story that I heard from a Holocaust survivor who told me how his father always gave his ration of food to him and eventually died of starvation. The father gave to fulfill the need of his son at the expense of his own life.

When we see someone give to us in this way, we understand that the giver gets great satisfaction from seeing us more fulfilled. When we experience altruistic love, we come into contact with the reality and worth of our personhood. We feel both lifted up and humbled by such giving.

We not only have a need to feel that we are special or unique and that we are not alone in our journey of life, but we also have the need for *meaning* that our personhood is worth a great deal to someone. This feeling is usually very natural with our children, but it should also be clearly present in our marriage.

So, how do we define marital love? Perhaps this is the place to start: *Love is a giving of adoration, companionship, and sacrifice for the spouse's good.*

Trust

Love does so many wonderful things for people, but again, it is not the whole story in marriage. Trust is the other essential in relationships and there is reason to believe that trust is even more important than love. Trust has been identified as being a much greater predictor of marital outcome than is love (Jacobson & Margolin, 1979). Trust does not get as much press in marital therapy, or in popular culture, so lay people and therapists are even more confused about what trust entails.

If I am more partial to one particular family therapy theory than others, it would have to be Contextual Family Therapy (Boszormenyi-Nagy & Krasner, 1986). Contextual theory has a sound foundation for explaining trustworthiness as an essential element in making relationships work because it allows relational partners to give to each other in a responsible and reliable manner. At the heart of this theory is the belief that we are built in such a way that as we interact in relationships, we have an innate sense of justice that demands that we try to balance what we are entitled to receive and what we are obligated to give in order to maintain the relationship. In very simple terms, in every relationship, we are entitled to take something for ourselves and are obligated to give something back. The give-and-take in a relationship should be balanced so that the relationship is fair. The interdependence of a spousal relationship requires us to assume responsibility for our actions, to accept the consequences of how we carry out the relationship, and to strive for fairness and balance in the relationship's give-and-take.

The balance of this obligation (give) and merit (take) can be illustrated by setting them up like a bookkeeping account in a ledger. Figure 1.1 shows a relational ledger for a husband and wife. The left side of the ledger account represents the merit (take) that a spouse is entitled to receive from his or her partner: respect, care, and spousal intimacy. The spouse is entitled to these things partly because that is what husbands and wives provide in our society, but mostly because he or she is expected, or obligated, to give those same things to his or her spouse. On the right side of the ledger, the spouse's obligations (give) that maintain the relationship are listed. Here you find the same obligation to provide what he or she is entitled to receive. The relationship is balanced, symmetrical, and fair, as the spouses give to each other.

Merit or Take	Obligations or Give
(What Individuals Are Entitled to)	(What Individuals Are Obligated to Give)
1. Respect	1. Respect
2. Care	2. Care
3. Intimacy	3. Intimacy

Figure 1.1 The Spousal Ledger

When there is this type of balance between giving what the relationship requires and receiving that to which spouses are entitled, the sense of fairness is satisfied. As this balance between give-and-take continues over time, spouses experience trustworthiness in each other. As we experience trust, we are enabled to give to the other. In other words, as I do my part in my relationship with my wife and she does hers, I give freely because I trust that she will give me what I need. I do not have to threaten her or manipulate her to get it. When my trust level is high, I work on fulfilling *my* obligations because I am confident that my justified needs will be met.

So how spouses fulfill their obligations to each other will dictate, in large part, how much they trust one another. If trust is high in the relationship, then the spouses will feel relaxed in their giving to meet their obligations. They know their spouses will reciprocate in a responsible way and thus both will get what they need. However, when trust disappears, spouses cannot give freely because they are always worried that their spouses will take advantage of them and will not meet their needs in return. When trust is low, spouses withhold and the relationship is perceived as less trustworthy. As spouses get less and less of what they feel entitled to, they give less and less and they become more aggressive in trying to force the other to do his or her part. This downward spiral of destructive action and counteraction effectively kills off the giving in the relationship and eventually kills off "us."

This framework actually provides a very effective tool for understanding emotions. When relationships are put into this context of fairness regarding give-and-take, we can see that the sense of justice or balance is key. Emotions are simple barometers that give us a reading on the status of balance between relational give and relational take. When spouses do not receive what they deserve, they become angry. On the other hand, when spouses benefit too much from relationships in which they are not doing their fair share, they feel guilty. These basic emotions of anger and guilt, and their various shades and intensities, motivate all sorts of further destructive actions, such as threats, manipulation, violence, addictions, neglect, withdrawal, and divorce.

Although trustworthiness helps to foster relationship satisfaction, it is not a static resource. It is either accrued or depleted in relationships. You can see how this works in the example of the husband and wife that I use in my seminars and have written about before (Hargrave, 2000). For example, say my wife wanted to go to a secluded mountain cabin for a few months to write a novel. She would be neither with the family or contributing to the relationship. The responsibility for the care of the family would fall on me. However, because we have had many years of balanced and fair relating, I would support my wife's decision to go. Simply put, I trust her and I believe that she would do the same for me if I were to make such a request. A large reserve of trust would enable the relationship to continue as it was, even though there would be an imbalance for several months. Without that reservoir of trust, it would be very difficult for me to support her.

As I mentioned, trust is a fluid attribute. Because there is enough trust in reserve to get us through one transition does not mean that it will never be a problem. For instance, if after three months, my wife were to ask for another three months, I might agree, but not nearly so willingly. If, at the end of this period, she did not call and I had to search for her, my trust resource likely would be totally depleted. I would feel that I was being denied my relationship entitlement and I would withhold anything more. Giving would be replaced with threats and other destructive responses. Trust is built and maintained by fair exchange. When the exchange rate gets out of balance, trust crumbles and the relationship becomes endangered.

The key element of trust *is the ability to give freely to another believing that the other will responsibly and reliably give back.* This sense of reciprocation and mutuality allows the "us" relationship to have goals and direction.

Stability, Security, and Sincerity

Just as individuals move through developmental stages—physically, intellectually, and emotionally—so does the "us" relationship. People have to go through childhood and adolescence, and so does their "us." Just as there is controversy about how to raise the brightest and best-adjusted children, so there are many different opinions on how to create the best type of relationship. In child rearing, most approaches have the same type of goals in mind for children. We want kids to be self-confident, self-assured, stable, disciplined, emotionally connected, and growing. The same is true of various marriage therapies. We want to see marriages that are stable, intimate, and nurturing, and that foster growth in the relational partners.

As a therapist, I want couples to develop a solid "us" relationship. I know that essential to making the "us" strong is making the relationship loving and trustworthy. I also realize that building a loving and trustworthy relationship is something that takes time, especially when a couple's "us-ness" has been severely damaged by unloving and untrustworthy actions. How do we as therapists go about guiding partners in the work of reconstructing "us" relationships?

There are three guiding attitudes that I work on in couples therapy: stability, security, and sincerity. I see these attitudes as somewhat developmental and sequential and believe that they can encapsule this important work. These attitudes guide the therapeutic work and chart the necessary goals in therapy. I do not offer these attitudes or this therapeutic approach as the "only" way to do therapy, nor do I believe that it makes other therapies obsolete. As a therapist, I am always looking for ways to give my work clarity and direction so that my patients can get the best help possible. This approach is the result of my efforts.

Stability

Stability is the state in which a couple is assured of a safe, nonthreatening, and nondestructive relationship. Partners cannot express their deepest thoughts and fears to each other if the information is going to be misused in some way. Stability is the attitude that spouses must achieve if they are to live together without hurting each other individually.

Achieving stability is a primary goal for new couples and couples who have been destructive to one another. Individual family-of-origin issues and established conflict styles are among the common factors that can interfere with stability. Helping a couple to achieve stability in the relationship involves a humbling process for both partners in which they also become more respectful of their spouse.

Security

Security is a place that encompasses commitment, reliability, and responsibility in a relationship and grows love and trust. After the partners are reasonably assured that they will not attack each other's individuality and that they can live together as an "us" in a nondestructive way, the question becomes one of whether the couple can carry out the activities of life in such a way that builds their intimacy together. Security is the attitude that assures the couple that they are headed in the same direction and that they can face both easy and hard issues and still come out together. When the relationship is insecure, the partners are at odds, frustrating each other's individual goals in the important activities of marriage, such as finances, child rearing, household management, and work. If they don't feel secure in how "us" will handle such issues, they tend to start separating and competing for power. If this competition is left unchecked, soon the "us-ness" of the relationship deteriorates and the partners head in separate directions.

Security is a primary factor for couples that are past the newly married stage but not quite into the middle years of marriage. Most couples deal with security issues between the second and seventh years of marriage. It is a crucial time in which it becomes apparent whether a couple will consolidate their "us" identity together, or whether they will pull apart and be individuals outside of the relationship.

Sincerity

Sincerity reflects the ability to learn about one's self and achieve personal growth in the context of the marital relationship. As partners give to each other in the close context of marriage, they begin to genuinely experience the satisfaction that comes from it. The intense warmth and peacefulness that come from sacrificing personal wants or desires for the sake of a partner's wants and desires are unlike any other. They begin to see mutual sacrifice as a way of personal fulfillment and the marital "us-ness" as a means to promote and support each other. It is common in my experience that partners who have been married for years are happiest when they see their partner successful. It is not a matter of being codependent; rather, it is a matter of the "us" becoming so strong that the individual partners share in each other's triumphs and failures and want to make sacrifices.

But sincerity not only includes sacrificial giving, it also means being willing to give up the part of individuality that is infantile or selfish. Marriage is particularly powerful in its ability to point out our stubborn and immature attitudes. If marriage is to do its work on us as individuals, we have to be sincere and honest enough to admit to these shortcomings and change.

Where one partner is unwilling to sacrifice to see the other partner succeed, or is not inclined to change for the sake of the relationship, Insincerity is the result. Couples will be dishonest and defensive as they seek to maintain their dysfunction and selfishness. Instead of sacrificing for each other's goals, they will connive to achieve their own objectives.

In essence, sincerity is the ability of each partner to grow individually because of the relationship instead of at the relationship's expense. This attitude is important throughout marriage, but seems to become more and more essential as a couple matures through the first and second decade of being together.

Conclusions

Why do marriages get into trouble? They do so because the partners have lost the essential quality of what they are together—"us." People want to be fulfilled, that is a given. Fulfillment for many lies in a significant relationship. What makes for a healthy relationship? The elements of mutual love and trust help to grow healthy individuals. These elements are also integral to healthy relationships that are intimate and nurturing. As therapists, we have the opportunity to help couples to develop loving and trustworthy "us" relationships and to work on therapeutic attitudes that achieve the goals of stability, security, and sincerity.

chapter two

The Realities of Marriage and Marital Therapy

Will the institution of marriage survive? This is often a question in today's society. On one side are the conservatives who see marriage as being in serious trouble and believe its deterioration has led to the demise of the family. The logic goes that unstable families produce children and adults who are more apt to have trouble adjusting to society's norms and have a greater propensity for irresponsibility, rebellion, and even criminal behavior. On the other side of the issue, we find more liberal types who see marriage as an old institution in need of serious modification to cope with the stresses of modern living. This line of thinking holds that the old ideas of marriage are inadequate to meet contemporary societal demands and that it is this inadequacy that is at the root of our difficulty with adjustment and growth.

Of course, both arguments have some merit, but more truth is found in the balance between the two than in either one alone. Increasingly, the literature has offered compelling evidence that deteriorating marriages are bad for children and adults alike (Amato & Booth, 1997; Whitehead, 1996) and that this deterioration can be linked to undesirable antisocial attitudes (Amato & Booth, 1997). Clearly, our social structure has also produced a stressful environment in which rigid and patriarchal forms of family do not have the flexibility to meet the financial, emotional, or social needs of many individuals. The institution of marriage thus must become responsible in meeting the relational needs of both children and adults and it must be flexible enough to meet the demands of society. William Doherty (1992) has pointed out this need for families to become more intentional in being more flexible while still maintaining responsibility.

The question, however, may not be whether or not marriage will survive, but *how it will survive*. Getting married is one of our most popular voluntary actions as we enter adulthood and over 90% of people will marry at some time in their lives (Glick, 1989). In spite of all the forecasts of doom for the family, the negative perceptions of marriage, and the 50% divorce rate (U.S. Bureau of the Census, 1995), people still get married. Even with the phenomenal rise in cohabitation, which stood at 3.5 million in 1993 (U.S. Bureau of the Census, 1994) and is now estimated to include over four million people, marriage still is the ultimate goal for most. Marriage, it seems, *will* survive, but *how* it will survive remains a significant question for therapists and couples alike. Will it survive by being a primary relationship of contention and unhappiness? Will it survive by having marital partners divorce each other to marry others in a search for "the right spouse"? Or will it survive by binding spouses legally, but with no emotional connection?

The answer, we hope, is "none of the above." Both couples and therapists want marriages to embody love and trust. They want marriages that have a sense of relational "us-ness," that can handle conflict, that are able to deal with the complexities of life, and that can promote individual and relational growth. In short, as therapists and as couples, we should want marriages to be strong "us" relationships that are stable, secure, and sincere.

How, then, do we help couples get to this place that they and we want them to reach? Even though the field of marriage and family therapy as a whole, and marital therapy specifically, has been slow in evolving helpful outcome research, there are some important things that we can learn from what has been produced. We can use what we know from a scientific viewpoint to be more helpful in our work as clinicians. Therefore, the following sections review some important findings from the literature as a basis for understanding the therapeutic intent of moving marriages toward being stable, secure, and sincere.

Types of Marriages

One helpful way to understand marriage is to recognize that not all marriages have the same problems and strengths. There are important qualitative differences in the relational patterns of couples that can be understood by grouping or typing marital relationships. One of the best researched and most helpful typologies of marriages is that developed by Fowers and Olson (1993). These typologies were developed from data gathered from the analysis of the marital inventory ENRICH, which is a self-report instrument that each spouse answers separately. The inventory measures marital satisfaction by analyzing the couple's agreement in 10 relational areas: personality issues, communication, conflict resolution, financial management, leisure activities, sexual relationship, children and parenting, family and friends, role relationship, and spiritual beliefs.

Vitalized Marriages

In vitalized marriages, spouses have a high degree of relational satisfaction. They report a high level of comfort in discussing their feelings and in communicating with each other, and have the ability to resolve conflict. They indicate a high level of satisfaction with how they relate to each other in activities and in expressing their sexual desires. They also agree for the most part on how they handle financial and parenting issues and on their preference for egalitarian role patterns.

Harmonious Marriages

Spouses in a harmonious marriage report a moderate degree of relationship satisfaction and have a reasonable ability to communicate feelings and resolve conflicts. They have reasonably strong sexual feelings toward each other and do well in terms of agreeing on financial issues, but not so well regarding parenting issues. Spiritual matters do not play a large role in the relationship.

Traditional Marriages

In traditional marriages, spouses report a moderate level of dissatisfaction with the personal habits of their partners, feel less comfortable with sharing feelings, and have more difficulty in resolving conflict. These couples find greater satisfaction and show more strength in dealing with parenting issues and have a high agreement on spiritual beliefs, but are less strong and find less satisfaction when dealing with individual and couple emotional dynamics. However, they show a high sense of direction with regard to the activities of marriage.

Conflicted Marriages

Conflicted marriages produce dissatisfaction in a number of areas. Spouses in these marriages report dissatisfaction with the personal habits of their partners, do not feel comfortable with expressing their feelings to each other, and cannot resolve conflict on a consistent basis. They have difficulty with planning, such as making decisions regarding finances and parenting, and they have a low degree of sexual satisfaction.

Devitalized Marriages

In devitalized marriages, the spouses experience tremendous relational dissatisfaction in every area. They dislike the personal habits of their spouses, do not share feelings or communicate openly, and do not resolve conflict. There is very little agreement on leisure activities, financial issues, or parenting, and little satisfaction with the sexual relationship. Spiritual beliefs play a very small role in the relationship.

Stability, Security, Sincerity, and Marriage Typology

These typologies of marital relationships enable therapists to understand important aspects of what is happening in marriages. Couples in vitalized marriages, we might hypothesize, have a strong couple identity. They feel emotionally connected to and understood by their spouses and hold them in high regard. This internal dynamic of connection and appreciation could be interpreted as a high degree of love for each other. In addition, these couples have had good experiences in working out and planning the activities and obligations of the relationship with regard to financial planning, parenting, and the division of tasks. This satisfaction could be interpreted as a high degree of marital trust. In these loving and trusting relationships, the satisfaction is high and, therefore, the relationship is both stable and secure. It would be logical to assume that these spouses see their marriage as strengthening their personal growth and as leading them to greater sincerity as the relationship deepens.

Vitalized couples seldom seek therapy because they have the ability to use their relationship as a learning tool. The rare instances where they do ask for a therapist's help generally relate to a specific decision or circumstance that the couple recognizes as causing undue conflict or stress. When such situations arise, the vitalized couple will opt for shorter-term therapy that calls on their resources of stability, security, and sincerity. As a result, their therapy is usually relatively brief, as well as highly successful.

Harmonious couples will seek therapy for a variety of issues, ranging from specific stress caused by financial or parenting conflict to overall relational unhappiness. These couples have some ability to work out internal emotional connections, but it is not as nearly as strong as with vitalized couples. The spouses probably love each other, but are not particularly appreciative of or excited by their partner. They have been able to solve problems with regard to the activities of marriage, but have also experienced difficulties in staying together. As a result, a harmonious couple has likely established a fairly consistent baseline of stability in the relationship, but is not as together or secure as the others in dealing with the issues of life. Thus, these couples are unlikely to feel a high degree of relational "us-ness" and do not experience as much sincere individual and couple growth as does a vitalized couple.

Harmonious couples do not have a traditional role structure and do not usually have spiritual beliefs that guide them away from divorce. In therapy, therefore, these couples will be much more likely to have individual interests apart from the relationship and less restrictive thoughts about separation and divorce. It becomes essential, then, to help them to use their moderate resources and strengths in being emotionally connected to develop a more consistent pattern of security in dealing with marital activities. In addition, the harmonious couple needs assistance in nurturing the relational identity of "us" in order to learn how to grow together.

In some ways, traditional couples are the reverse of harmonious couples. Traditional couples have less ability for, and find less satisfaction in, emotional connection and communication, but are more consistent in dealing with the activities of marriage. In other words, the emotional connection of love between the spouses may be weaker, but the trustworthiness in dealing with activities is high. This makes for a more secure relationship in that the couple can trust each other to accomplish marital activities, but it also makes for a less stable environment as the couple experiences less appreciation and affection, and more anger. There is security in the relationship, but greater instability.

The spouses in traditional marriages usually have fairly rigidly defined roles, as well as spiritual beliefs that preclude separation or divorce. As a result, these partners usually stay together because the relationship is secure. However, they will be very unstable with regard to how they handle personal and communication issues. Very few traditional couples have a strong sense of relational "us-ness." They are trustworthy, but usually not loving. This makes the possibility for sincerity, or individual and marital growth, very low. These couples often seek therapy because they are so dissatisfied with the status of emotional connection in the marriage. The therapy must entail establishing a couple identity by using their security resources to start building stability and closeness.

Couples in both conflicted and devitalized marriages have very low relational resources. They are emotionally disconnected, which indicates very little love in the relationship, and they consistently work against each other in the activities of marriage, which almost always results in a lack of trust. In these types of marriages, there is little sense of relationship, but just two individuals existing, and usually competing, with one another.

Such couples usually bring to therapy a multitude of issues that indicate instability, insecurity, and insincerity. For the therapy to succeed, the couple identity with regard to love and trust must be constructed step-by-step. First, the couple must be taught to stabilize the relationship by not indulging in destructive conflict. Second, the couple must learn to deal with the activities of marriage in a cooperative and trustworthy way. If these first two steps are accomplished successfully, then the therapy can proceed to help the couple recognize mutual giving and growth. With this type of couple, of course, therapy is usually complex and longer term.

Predictors of Marital Success

Olson and DeFrain (1997) suggest several commonsense predictors of marital success, among them: shared companionship, love, and intimacy; support for each other; and the ability to have a satisfying sexual relationship. But these characteristics of a successful marriage are not natural endowments for many couples, which has led marital therapists and researchers to conclude that achieving marital success takes work.

Since the 1970s, there has been a movement among marital therapists to teach marriage as a skill. Some of the better known school-based programs are: "Building Relationships" developed by Life Innovations, Inc., based on Olson and DeFrain's research; "Connections" developed by Charlene Kamper and published by the Dibble Fund; and "Practical Exercises Enriching Relationship Skills" based on the work of Lori Gordon and published by the PAIRS Foundation, Inc. These programs all emphasize effective communication and problem solving, understanding and resolving conflict, and understanding relationships, as well as training for life skills. Other programs are premarital, designed to help individuals prepare for the demands and rigors of marriage. They include "PREPARE" developed by Olson, Fournier, and Druckman (1989), and the "Prevention Relationship Enrichment Program" or PREP, developed by Renick, Blumberg, and Markman (1992). Again, these courses seek to identify various types of information, such as communication and conflict issues, and guide the couple to constructive behavioral ways to improve marital skills.

The programs are designed in the belief that if individuals develop the necessary skills, the chances for marital success will be greater. Skill building has been a major focus for many of the marital therapy programs, and in much of the literature as well. Among the better-known programs are the "Practical Application of Intimate Relationship Skills" or PAIRS (Gordon, 1990) and PREP (Markman, Stanley, & Blumberg, 1994). Skill-building approaches in marital therapy include "Behavioral Marital Therapy" or BMT (Jacobson & Margolin, 1979) and Imago therapy, based on the approach developed by Hendrix (1988). These programs and therapies also utilize communication and conflict skill training, as well as a variety of ways to identify and deal with family-of-origin issues to enrich activities, and to resolve sexual problems.

From the viewpoint of a skill-based approach, what are predictors of marital success? Sperry and Carlson (1991) have suggested 10 character-istics of satisfying marriages that sum up these approaches well. Satisfying marriages are ones in which partners accept individual respon-sibility for their behavior and self-esteem, align their personal and marital goals, encourage each other, communicate their feelings openly and hon-estly, listen empathically, and seek to understand outside factors that influence their relationship. They also demonstrate acceptance of each other, choose positive words and actions, solve marital conflicts, and commit themselves to equality in the marriage. It is easy to see from this list that the goals of skill programs and therapy would be to enlighten spouses about their behavior and teach them the necessary skills to acquire these characteristics.

Skill-based programs are certainly logical. If couples are finding it dif-ficult to achieve marital satisfaction, that difficulty should be traceable to a cause. As therapists or educators, we should be able to root out the cause and replace it with more adaptable behavior. This is good logic, but as we pointed out previously, education is not always the answer.

John Gottman, the world's premier marital researcher, has spent over 20 years ferreting out what makes marriages work and what makes them fail. His approach is scientific and helps us identify the positive and negative aspects of marriage. He and his research associates have been able to identify spouses who will eventually divorce with an accuracy of 94% (Gottman, 1994). Skills are important of course, but what Gottman has consistently found is that a couple's attitudes and efforts are of equal significance.

Gottman, for example, noted that every couple has conflicts, and that there are three primary styles in dealing with them: validation, avoidance, and volatility. Spouses who validate meet their conflicts head on and work them out to their mutual satisfaction, whereas conflict-avoiding spouses agree that they will disagree and seldom resolve their problems. Volatile marriage partners deal with conflicts by engaging in passionate disputes. Skill-based programs and therapy would suggest that validation would be the "healthiest" way to deal with conflict and that the other two would lead to serious marital difficulties. However, according to Gottman's research, all three response types are equally stable and none should be singled out as a predictor of divorce. Instead, what he discov-ered was that *positivity* was the essential element in dealing with conflict constructively. Spouses who were able to handle conflict, no matter their style, exhibited positive feelings much more often than they did negative ones. They did get angry, but their positive behavior—being interested, affectionate, caring, appreciative, concerned, empathetic, and accepting—outweighed the negative behavior. Gottman also found that those who were able to deal with conflict in a positive way were anxious to address the disagreement and move on.

Predictors of
Dissatisfaction and Dissolution

Marriages do not just fall into the ditch of dissatisfaction; rather, they begin a relatively slow decline that picks up speed as things get worse. Gottman (1994) has used his same scientific approach in identifying the predictors of marital problems and divorce. He developed what he refers to as the "four horsemen of the apocalypse" as a means of recognizing the warning signs in problem marriages. The four—criticism, contempt, defensiveness, and stonewalling—are somewhat sequential in nature. In other words, criticism tends to lead to contempt, contempt to defensiveness, and so on. Once these four "horsemen" appear in a couple's interactions, the marriage begins a distinct downward spiral toward dissolution. Knowledge of these predictors allows us to understand what we must prevent if we are going to be helpful to couples in therapy.

Criticism

Criticism involves attacking another's personality or character. This is different from complaining, which Gottman claims to be one of the more functional behaviors in marriage, in that complaining means pointing out one's dissatisfaction with a specific behavior. We can clearly see the difference between a spouse's saying to his or her partner, "I don't like it when you don't balance the checkbook," and "You are the most irresponsible person that I've ever met. What is wrong with you?" But that difference isn't always so clear. For instance, if a spouse complains about too many unsatisfactory behaviors at one time, or brings up the same ones again and again, the partner is likely to feel criticized. Also, if complaints are generalized ("It frustrates me because you have trouble completing projects"), they tend to be taken as criticism.

Contempt

It is easy to slide from complaint into criticism as frustration and anger are involved. But criticism, especially criticism that continues, puts spouses on a course for meeting Gottman's second horseman, the one he labels "contempt." Contempt is the *intention* to insult or psychologically abuse one's partner. When spouses feel contempt for each other, they hurl insults and call each other names. Contempt also includes the use of sarcastic humor and mockery, and generally making hurtful fun of a spouse. Gottman also has identified contemptuous body language, primarily involving facial expressions. Sighing heavily, sneering, rolling one's eyes, and pulling at or curling the upper lip all communicate contempt or disgust.

One of the reasons that contempt is so damaging to marital relationships is that it seems to negate any positive feeling that the spouses might have for each other. As I have pointed out, Gottman (1994) identifies positivity as one of the primary contributors to marital stability. As positive feelings erode and are replaced by criticism and contempt, couples start the process of attacking each other *with the intent of hurting*. Once they reach this stage of intent, the stability of the marriage is threatened and any possibility of security or sincerity disappears.

Defensiveness

Gottman (1994) points to self-defensiveness as the natural response to criticism and contempt. But the problem with defensiveness is that each spouse begins to see himself or herself as right and the partner as the problem. Spouses resist their partner's influence blocking any communication that seems at all threatening. Gottman identifies several defensive behaviors, including denying responsibility, making excuses, cross-complaining, automatically disagreeing, and accusing the accuser of the same behavior.

In the broadest sense, I believe there are two primary ways in which one can be defensive. One is to react *passively* and ignore the criticism and contempt as the mere rantings and ravings of a lunatic, not worthy of an active response. Another way to be defensive is to become the *aggressor* and attack the criticizing partner with angry words and accusations. In the aggressive approach, the one criticized vigorously disagrees with anything the other says, complains and criticizes, in return, and cross-accuses the critical spouse. But whether passive or aggressive, defensiveness tends only to escalate the conflict. If spouses feel that their frustrations and complaints are not being addressed, their frustration and anger grows, resulting in further criticism and expressions of contempt. It is like the saying in family therapy, "If people try something in a relationship that they believe should work and it doesn't, they will just try the same thing harder." The same is true of marriages. When spouses have critical, contemptuous quarrels that do not result in getting the frustration and anger worked out of the relationship, they most often will go on to have an even more critical and more contemptuous quarrel. Defensiveness guarantees the escalation of problems.

When defensiveness becomes a pattern in marriages, I believe that it is a sure sign that trustworthiness has deteriorated to a critical point. When I am defensive, I am saying, in essence, that the problem does not lie with me, the problem is my spouse. I excuse myself from having a part in the problem and thereby excuse myself from having to make any effort to solve it. In short, I stop interacting and, more important, *I stop giving*. When a spouse stops doing his or her part, relationship is no longer in balance and whatever trustworthiness there was in the relationship no longer exists. When partners are consistently defensive, their marriages are surely unstable and insecure, and, therefore, not loving or trustworthy.

Stonewalling

Stonewalling is what the word implies. A marital partner becomes like a stone wall when the other partner tries to communicate. Gottman indicates that stonewalling usually occurs when relationships have been characterized by criticism, contempt, and defensiveness for some time, and that it is a clear signal that the couple is reaching the end of the relationship. It means that at least one of the marital partners has given up even trying to communicate in the marriage. When you see habitual stonewalling, it is as if the person is saying, "The marriage is hopeless, so why try to talk or straighten things out? They will just continue to get worse." Partners check out emotionally and are on the road to checking out of the marriage physically.

I believe that stonewalling is the precursor to the death of a marriage. When partners quit working actively on the relationship, they are murdering the "us-ness" in the relationship by denying it the love and trust that would ensure its survival. Once stonewalling is consistently present, the couple's relational "us" is gone and it becomes very difficult to resurrect positivity in the marriage.

Good Marriage or Bad Marriage?

One of the difficult issues in marital therapy is trying to determine whether a marriage is good or bad. Does a good marriage mean one in which conflict is low or the couple has never considered divorce? Most therapists would say No. We have done therapy with spouses who were in very unhappy situations but fully intended to stay together. However, much of the research on marriage outcomes has been focused on the ability of the couple to stay together or to reduce conflict.

Certainly the reduction of marital conflict does increase the likelihood that a couple will not divorce. An estimated 30% of couples who divorce are highly conflictual (Amato & Booth, 1997), and thus conflictual couples are the ones most likely to seek divorce (Fowers, Montel, & Olson, 1996). Several studies have shown that marital therapy can be effective, at least in the short term, in reducing conflict, and thus increasing marital satisfaction (Baucom & Hoffman, 1986; Dunn & Schwebel, 1995; Hahlweg & Markman, 1988; Jacobson & Addis, 1993). As suggested by Gottman and Gottman (1998), however, most of these positive results from these studies should not be attributed to the couples' marriages getting better as much as to the fact that the control couples' marriages continued to deteriorate. In other words, it may be possible that current marital therapy does not make the relationship better, but instead keeps it from worsening. Still, there is evidence (Jacobson, Schmaling, Holtzworth, & Monroe, 1987; Markman, Renick, & Floyd, 1993) that suggests that marital therapy and premarital training do have long-term positive outcomes in terms of an increase in marital satisfaction, the reduction of conflict, and a decrease in divorces among couples who enter therapy.

It makes sense that if a couple cannot achieve some sense of relational stability, the relationship will not be good or satisfying. Stability in marital relationships is like a foundation for a house. Although a solid foundation does not guarantee that the house it supports will be solid as well, if the foundation is unstable, it is impossible for the house itself to stand firm and strong. Likewise, a stable couple relationship in which conflict is handled in such a way that the spouses do not harm each other and resolve issues successfully does not guarantee marital satisfaction. However, if they cannot achieve stability in the relationship and are constantly in conflict, then their marital satisfaction is certain to be low.

It makes sense, then, that most of the research at this early stage in the history of marital therapy has focused on conflict and dissolution as the standard of effectiveness. Stability is indeed essential to marital success. But *stability* is different from *satisfaction*. The fact is that the quality of surviving marriages is very poor. Many such marriages report at least one partner as dissatisfied with the relationship. In one survey, over 40% of married people said they had considered leaving their partners, over 20% said that they were dissatisfied with their marriage most of the time, and 28% reported having previously been divorced (Gallup, 1989). Arond and Pauker (1987) found that among newlywed couples, 51% had doubts that their marriages would last and 45% were not satisfied with their sexual relationship. Many marriages that survive obviously are simply bad marriages.

How can we, as therapists, make relationships more satisfying for dissatisfied couples? If a couple has achieved some sense of stability and the partners are not threatening or damaging each other, they must be encouraged to pull together to work on their marriage in a reliable way. It is difficult for a couple to learn how to manage the activities of life, such as making enough money to support themselves and the family, raising their children, meeting work demands, providing for housing and transportation, and dealing with extended-family issues. There are no easy answers to offer or exact ways to move spouses to solve their problems. They must develop a sense of what works for them. Some couples, for instance, might be better off dividing household tasks, responsibility for income, and child-rearing duties between the spouses. Other couples might find it more advantageous for one spouse to earn most of the income while the other assumes the greater responsibility for taking care of the home. In either case, however, the spouses must learn how to work together, take their fair share of the responsibility, and then reliably carry out that responsibility. In short, the couple must develop a sense of security as well as stability.

Does achieving stability and security guarantee marital satisfaction? Again, we as therapists can easily say No. Indeed, 70% of divorcing couples are not highly conflictual (Amato & Booth, 1997). Thus, it can be assumed that even though the 70% are not involved in conflict, there is a high degree of dissatisfaction. Also, the inability to achieve stability and security increases the likelihood of dissatisfaction. Spouses who cannot carry out the activities of life as a couple will find themselves consistently disappointed and frustrated with each other. This will result in their attacking each other personally, which can cause the relational stability to disintegrate, or will impel each partner to drift into activities that he or she can accomplish individually without relying on the spouse. This, in turn, results in the partners' becoming alienated, leading separate lives like roommates, which eventually destroys any emotional connection.

It is the mutual cooperation and achievement of security that set the stage for a strong couple sincerity. Remember that sincerity in marriage is about individual and relational growth through giving and learning. Spouses in stable and secure marriages do not harm one another in their conflicts and are able to achieve goals and manage activities together. The next step is for them to grow closer together by making sacrifices so that the other might achieve his or her desires and so become healthier as individuals. This growth component has been largely neglected as an essential element in the context of marital therapy. Although it is harder to conceptualize how to teach couples to grow in a relationship than it is to teach them how to listen to each other effectively, such growth is the final element constituting a satisfying marriage.

Do stability, security, and sincerity guarantee marital satisfaction? I believe that the answer is Yes. Good marriages do not just result from the fact that there is reduced conflict or simply because the marriages have survived. Good marriages are not just those in which the couple is able to work together. But where couples are safe, able to accomplish the tasks of life, and grow toward individual and couple goals, it is safe to say that their marriages are good.

The Process of Therapy

As clinicians, we are familiar with what marriage entails, and certainly with the process of marital therapy. However, there are some couples who come to therapy with problems that initially appear overwhelming. Remember, these couples are lost in a confusing maze and are looking to us, as therapists, to direct them to the right path and help them deal with the confusion. No matter what therapeutic process we utilize, if we are to be helpful to these couples, we have to rely on what we know and translate it into direction and guidelines for making the marriage successful. In trying to translate what I know about good relationships in order to be helpful to couples, I have followed a logical progression in my thinking about the process of therapy.

The Goal

We are trained by our academic institutions and directed by insurance companies to deduce the therapeutic goals from our patients' statements. But, as I have stated before, most couples are not really clear on what marriage is or what it is supposed to be. I may hear vague statements from the spouses, such as, "I want to solve my marital problems," or "I want to have a good marriage," but the partners are not clear about what it means to achieve that goal.

After some initial joining with the couple and learning something of the processes and problems of their relationship, I make it a point to give them a clear idea of the goal of marital therapy. I do this by outlining the expectations of what marriage can, and should, be. The first goal of marital therapy is to *develop a strong "us" relationship and identity that both partners will experience as loving, trustworthy, and growing.*

When I explain the concept of "us-ness" and why it is a desirable goal in marriage, very few couples disagree. However, there are those who nevertheless believe that it is a goal that is not achievable for them. This is understandable, especially for partners who have found their relationship a miserable, damaging, and hateful experience. I continue to state this high goal, however, because the couple will need to set their sights on a marriage that will be satisfying. Anything less than a loving, trustworthy, and growing marriage will short change that marital satisfaction. Research has also established that couples with high expectations for their marriages are more likely to achieve marital satisfaction (Gottman & Gottman, 1998).

I describe the idea of "us-ness" in a variety of ways, but it is also helpful for the couple do some thinking about the character of their relationship. Following is one of the exercises I prescribe to help a couple identify with their "us" relationship.

ᕙ *Couple Exercise One*

The "Us" Relationship Is the Key

Individual Versus Relational Needs

We live in an individualistic society. Look at all those messages we receive from society, from the media, from the people in our lives that tell us that we are rugged individuals and that we need to look out for ourselves.

- You have a right to say exactly what you feel.
- You must pursue in life what is right for you.
- You have a right to your personal happiness.
- You cannot live according to others' expectations, you gotta be you.

When relationships are loving, trustworthy, and growing, they take on personalities of their own. Think about your marriage. Chances are that it is not quite like you and not quite like your spouse. It is something more than either of you. You can probably assign such attributes to the relationship as "easygoing" and "unpredictable." These are all evidence (even though invisible) that the relationship is a living being.

The "food and water" essentials that keep relationships alive are love, trust, and growth. If love and trust are not present, a relationship will eventually weaken and die. Although it is important for you not to lose your identity, you must be willing to give up part of yourself in a loving, trustworthy way to keep the relationship alive. You must learn to balance what is good for you as an individual and what is good for the relationship.

Reasons for Relationships

Relationships are not designed to fulfill our personal needs or ensure our happiness. They are built for our personal growth and sacrifice. Two things keep relationships alive and growing: love and trust.

> *Love* is a giving of adoration, companionship, and sacrifice for the other's good.

> *Trust* is the ability to give to another freely because you believe that person will responsibly give to you what you need.

So when you create a marriage relationship, you are actually sacrificing part of your individuality (and your own selfishness) to give to your spouse and to receive, in turn, what he or she gives to you.

When this loving sacrifice is mutual and you can trust your spouse, the feeling is peaceful contentment in being able to rely on the relationship and grateful love for your spouse's personhood.

1. What are some of the characteristics of your current marital relationship?
2. What are some characteristics that you would like to be descriptive of your marriage?
3. As you currently function, are you more focused on your individuality or on the relationship? (Note that if you are just sacrificing your own desires for what your spouse wants, you are not focused on the relationship. The relationship is what is good for you and your spouse together, not what is good for your spouse.)
4. What are some things that each of you could do (be sure to focus on yourself and not on what your spouse could do) that would be good for the marriage?

As a therapist, I usually find it helpful to characterize the marriage according to the typology discussed above (Fowers & Olson, 1993). This typology gives me a picture of what the couple "us-ness" is like in its current form and an idea of the resources that are available to the couple. I often administer the ENRICH self-report instrument to a couple (available through Life Innovations). After each couple completes the inventory, the ENRICH is computer scored. Part of the information gleaned is the typology that fits the couple best.

However, I usually can tell what type of marriage the couple's "us-ness" has by the spouses' descriptions of themselves. If they are highly involved with each other, both verbally and nonverbally, and report satisfaction with each other and success in meeting obligations, then I can usually count on their being a vitalized couple. If the partners are generally satisfied with each other, but their difficulty in fulfilling mutual expectations and obligations is beginning to have a deleterious effect on the relationship, I am usually dealing with a harmonious couple. When a couple reports a high rate of success in accomplishing goals and meeting obligations but is fairly disconnected emotionally and has difficulty communicating, I assume that the couple has a traditional marriage. If the partners report being dissatisfied with each other and unable to cooperate in accomplishing goals, I know that they are either devitalized or conflicted. I have found that conflicted couples usually have more open and aggressive conflict, but are still working on the marriage and are trying to make it better. Devitalized couples are usually doing more stonewalling and are more likely to feel less enthusiastic about the marriage.

The path to this loving, trustworthy, and growing marriage is the therapeutic process of achieving stability, security, and sincerity. With a highly conflictual couple, the next therapeutic goal would be to attain stability in the relationship. Security, or learning how to work together, may be a therapeutic goal with a harmonious marriage whereas sincerity may be the goal with a more traditional couple. If a couple is unstable, insecure, and insincere, I usually try to set goals in sequence, starting with stability. But in all cases, the therapy must have all three goals of stability, security, and sincerity in order for love, trust, and growth to flourish in marriage. In communicating this to the couple, I try to explain the balance of the three, while pointing out which of the goals we will focus on first.

The Therapist's Role

I have heard both beginning and experienced therapists give responses that must cause patients to wonder why they came to therapy. A patient explains a situation to an empathetic and encouraging therapist: "I'm confused and don't know what to do. What do you think I should do?" The therapist's unhesitating response: "What do you think you should do?" Now I understand the value of reflection in helping a patient to gain insight and self-understanding, but most of the time, therapists use this answer to deflect their own responsibility. I have a general bias in that I believe that people usually seek therapy because they do not have the resources that they need to solve their problems on their own. That's why I feel rather frustrated with therapists who wait for their patients to set the therapeutic direction and are hesitant to give them honest answers.

This is especially true in marital therapy. The partners know that something is wrong, but have had no training and certainly have little intuition to tell them what is wrong or what they need to do to fix it. Saying what they feel and doing what comes naturally is what landed most of these couples in therapy in the first place. I believe, then, that the therapist must take the lead in charting the course for a good marriage in the same way that good guides make sure that their charges stay on the trail. The therapist must be very active in the therapy, willing to state the directions and goals, but also willing to stop destructive actions when spouses start attacking each other in harmful ways. But this does not mean that the therapist should take responsibility for the couple's marriage. The therapist needs to articulate clear guidelines and goals, be willing to demonstrate techniques and actions when needed, and confront and stop misguided behavior, but then has to assume the role of encourager and evaluator. In other words, the therapist can show the way and demonstrate how to get over the rough terrain, but he or she cannot make the couple do the work or do the work for them.

Reviews of therapy indicate that this type of directive approach is the most effective in helping couples change (Friedlander, Wildman, Heatherington, & Skowron, 1994). We do need to be good listeners and assist couples in doing some of their own reflection, but we also need to be willing to take risks and give direction to the therapy when couples need help. The approach need not be authoritarian: it can be respectful and collaborative as the therapist watches the couple and helps them to use the resources they already have to reach their goal of a good marriage.

Why People Come to Marital Therapy

The easy answer to why people come to marriage therapy is that they have a bad marriage. Specifically, people usually have struggling marriages because of some deficiency in the areas of stability, security, and sincerity. Any of these can impel a couple to seek therapy, and each produces particular characteristics or types of marital distress.

Lack of Stability

It is amazing to see how destructive spouses can be of each other. The insults they hurl, the manipulative and abusive things they do, and the physical violence they can perpetrate are astounding. Many couples want to try marital therapy because the spouses are locked into a war with each other and are actively engaged in a struggle to see who will win. What makes these situations so unstable is that in each spouse's view, the only way for the relationship to improve is for the other to give up his or her position of "rightness." In Gottman's (1994) terms, these couples are critical, contemptuous, and defensive.

Why do couples become so destructive? In my experience, there are two primary complicating factors behind instability. The first has to do with family background. Carl Whitaker use to quip that a family is formed when two scapegoats are sent out from their respective families to reproduce themselves. While some individuals we see may have been born into families that were truly positive and nurturing, many of our patients come from families in which they felt unloved and unwanted. When they depended on their families to give them messages of love, care, and nurture to assure them that they were unique, wanted, and precious, what they received instead was silence, messages of shame, or hostility. The result of this lack of love and trust was emotional conflicts for the children as they grew up trying to make sense of who they were, how they should act, and how to get what they missed in childhood. Many, and perhaps most, of these individuals grow up and marry partners whom they hope will provide them with a sense of identity and safety, and, in general, make up for what they lost in childhood. Of course, spouses are not equipped to do the job of parenting their partners, and they fail. When this happens, a spouse from a dysfunctional family background will often respond with a feeling of destructive rage and feel justified in manipulating or attacking the failed spouse. In these cases, the extreme destructive action is promoted by the fact that there were unsettled issues in the past that complicate and poison the present marriage. In Chapter 4, we discuss some of these family-of-origin issues in order to help spouses deal with the past in a beneficial and productive way.

The second complicating factor behind a lack of stability is often the conflict style of the couple. We all have different personalities and different ways of dealing with and operating in life. Sometimes a person will marry someone who is his or her opposite in personality or in the way that he or she manages life events. For instance, when faced with change, one partner may be very rigid , doing everything possible to avoid change and spending much time and effort on keeping everything stable and the same. If he or she were to marry a laid-back, or even chaotic, person, the prospect of change would create problems. Chaotic people consider change a fundamental part of life and see new and different ways as exciting or challenging. A chaotic person may want to change just for the sake of change because life is getting too predictable and boring. Even the simplest tasks would engender conflict, with both partners insisting on doing things his or her way. As a result, each move that the rigid spouse makes to ensure stability is met by a move by the chaotic spouse to promote change.

When there are opposite attitudes such as these, the conflicts tend to be symmetrical. In other words, both sides, rigid and chaotic, are equally powerful. In polar opposite or symmetrical conflicts, when one spouse makes an extreme statement or takes an extreme action, it provokes the other spouse to take an equally strong action or make an equally strong statement. When spouses have different personalities or ways of dealing with life, they often become critical and contemptuous of one another. The situation escalates, and continues to escalate, until the partners are constantly threatening each other and stability in the marriage is destroyed. In Chapter 5, we examine these polarized styles in depth to try to understand how to block the escalation and give stability a chance to grow.

Lack of Security
There are several tasks in marriage that can be divided between the

spouses in much the same way that the labor involved in producing an automobile can be divided. If adequate specifications and instructions are provided, a plant in Texas can assemble a transmission while a motor is being put together in Michigan and a body is being made in Canada. The parts can then be shipped to a central location where they will be combined to create a car. I have seen many couples who are able to divide a task, such as taking care of finances, and make it work. The spouses may have separate bank accounts, maintain their own investments, and take responsibility for paying certain bills. In these cases of divided tasks, however, the specifications and instructions regarding responsibilities must be very clear. Most couples, however, are not successful at allocating tasks, and of those who are, many do not have enough specific instructions concerning responsibility to ensure that the tasks are completed on schedule. Many couples just cannot learn how to do the work of marriage in responsible and reliable ways.

Tasks in marriage are simply the necessary routine in which the spouses learn how to trust and rely on each other. For example, even if they choose to keep their finances separate, there are significant areas where they must make financial decisions together, if only when deciding what food to buy. But most tasks require absolute cooperation and participation by both spouses. For instance, there cannot be successful parenting unless the parents both agree on how it should be done. How to share work and household responsibilities cannot be decided unilaterally when two people live under the same roof. And finally, sexual issues cannot be resolved by only one of the partners. Most of the tasks of marriage, such as dealing with finances, parenting, the extended family, gender issues, and sex, must be accomplished together.

Where there are tasks to be accomplished, the spouses must rely on each other to do his or her part. It is in the context of doing these tasks that they learn about giving and whether or not they can depend on each other. In short, these tasks give them the opportunity either to trust each other or not.

Spouses who come to therapy because of lack of security have learned that they cannot trust each other or are fearful that their inability to perform certain tasks will erode their trustworthiness. In Section III, we look in depth at the tasks whereby couples play out their relational trust. Issues of achieving security through responsible and reliable ways of dealing with money, gender, parenting, and sex are discussed.

Lack of Sincerity

Some couples come into therapy and we, as therapists, are tempted to ask, "What is the problem? You don't have terrible quarrels or disagreements. You have achieved most of your financial goals, live in a wonderful neighborhood, and have great children. I see many couples who are in trouble, but you two are okay." It is true that many therapists have made a career out of seeing patients who are in unstable and insecure marriages and so are at a loss when they encounter a marriage that suffers because of lack of sincerity, but it is important for therapists to realize that the issue of sincerity is just as painful for some couples as a lack of stability or security is for others.

Some couples have achieved stability and security in doing the work of marriage, but have lost touch with the *soul* of their marriage. Instead of being excited about each other's personhood and how each could contribute to the other's goals, they have forgotten, or lost touch with, the interests of their spouses. But more important, they often see the marital relationship and their spouse as uninterested in and uninvolved with their own lives. As a result, they themselves have become uninterested and uninvolved with the spouse. The marriage has ceased to grow and the spouses have quit using the relationship as a means to becoming well-rounded persons.

When spouses lose touch with each other, they come to therapy with two common complaints. The first complaint centers around boredom. When I hear this problem described by a spouse, he or she is usually telling me about how the other spouse is involved in his or her own activities, and ignores the complaining spouse or takes the spouse for granted. The spouse feels that the only purpose marriage serves is to pay the bills or raise the children, and has little emotional value for the partners. When the partners feel empty emotionally, the marriage follows the same dull routine of carrying out utilitarian functions. The second complaint usually centers around love. What I typically hear with this complaint is that a spouse is no longer romantically excited by his or her partner. This usually accompanies a long history of not being intimate, but along with it is the desire to be stimulated erotically.

In both complaints, the spouses are bemoaning the fact that the *intrinsic* value, the emotional connection of "us-ness," has been lost and that all that is left between them is everyday functioning. In both instances, the likelihood that one of the spouses will leave the marriage, have an affair, or pursue a career or hobby that doesn't include the other spouse is great. When spouses lose touch with sincerity, they start moving toward self-gratification, no matter what kind of stable and secure life they have built with their spouses.

Marriages go through various developmental stages and the needs that those stages present are very different for each stage. In many cases, marriages that lack sincerity have lasted for some time and the spouses have moved into a stage of life where they have tired of just meeting obligations. They want to be fulfilled emotionally and happier. The mistake that I see therapists make most often in working with these issues is that they try to act as a mediator of compromise so each partner can get a little of what he or she wants. Compromise is powerful, but many therapists tend to negotiate a settlement between individual spouses without paying enough attention to what is good for the relationship. When individuals complain of lack of emotional fulfillment and growth, they are saying the "us" relationship is faltering emotionally and is not functioning. Working to compromise their desires so that the spouses can get what they want in a self-protective way causes the relationship to weaken further and sets the couple on a course of competing for their own interests. In working with these lack-of-sincerity issues, it is necessary to move each spouse back into the relationship based on what he or she can give, not on what he or she can get. This, in turn, feeds the relationship and makes it stronger. Most important, since both spouses are giving to the "us" and each other through sacrifice and learning about themselves, *individual needs are met and the spouses are satisfied.* These ideas of how to work with sincerity issues are dealt with in Section IV.

The Process and Duration of Therapy

The course that the therapy takes depends, in large part, on the complexity of the problem that the couple brings in. There are exceptions, but I have found some consistent markers in the therapeutic process that give me a reasonable idea of how to proceed in marital therapy and of how much therapy will be helpful to the couple.

I feel that it is best to work on the marriage with both spouses present. If I am to discover the status of the "us" relationship, then I must see the "us" at work in the spouses' interactions and reactions. I do gather some individual family-of-origin material from each partner during therapy and do what would be considered individual work. But most times, I believe it is helpful for both spouses to be present to watch and listen. This usually allows each spouse to appreciate and understand his or her partner's situation and the forces that influence the relationship. There will be times when I see the spouses individually, but only for gathering the family-of-origin information and only for one or two sessions. I realize that because I see both spouses simultaneously, I may not get honest content information from the couple, especially at the beginning of therapy. But I believe that what I might lose in content, I more than make up for in learning about the couple's style and interaction. Generally, as therapy proceeds, I get much of the important content a couple is hesitant to reveal at first.

I believe that marital therapy can be broken down as follows: one or two sessions for evaluation; two to four sessions to ascertain the couple's type of marriage, style of conflict, and family-or-origin issues; two to three sessions to create an atmosphere for stability; three to five sessions to create an atmosphere for security; and one to three sessions to create an atmosphere for sincerity. This gives me a range of nine to 17 sessions of therapy. Many couples finish specific work in four to six sessions and a few may go beyond 17 sessions, but most will do the marital work necessary in these nine to 17 sessions. Even though my goal is for the couple to attain a loving, trustworthy, and growing "us" relationship, I realize that therapy is not the place where the couple lives. Therapy is intended to provide direction, evaluation, and practice for spouses working out individual and "us" issues, after which they return to their lives and apply what they have learned to real life. In other words, not all their problems will have been solved when they leave therapy, but the partners should have gained a clear idea of what to do to make their marriage a good marriage. When they run into confusing problems that they cannot solve for themselves, they will usually come back to therapy for one to four sessions to get some help. I find that telling couples how long I expect the therapy to take is usually helpful to them in setting their sights on achieving a good marriage.

Section II

Developing a Stable Atmosphere for "Us"

chapter three

Stability and Preventing Relational Damage

Imagine a couple in a rowboat, sitting side by side, each taking one of the oars. They believe that their boat is stable and secure and that they will have a wonderful journey together. They are happy for the companionship and deeply moved by the intimacy they share. They start rowing. Before long, each notices that the other rows differently. He or she is too slow or too fast, or doesn't get the oar deep enough in the water. Worse yet, he or she is constantly bragging about being a superior rower. The partners try to ignore the differences at first, but finally the time comes to try and "correct" the other's shortcomings. The partner responds by complaining and criticizing in turn. Soon the spouses stops paying attention to where they are heading and focus on how each partner is at fault. They become so frustrated that they start doing crazy things, like trying to humiliate the other into rowing the "right" way or physically trying to force the partner to acquiesce. They start nudging each other in disgust. The situation escalates and they push and shove. Eventually, they pull the oars out of the water and start flailing at one another.

The couple is not going anywhere, and they are doing each other tremendous physical and emotional damage. Couples sometimes start berating each other almost as soon as the marriage begins, sometimes out of frustration at not being able to fulfill marital expectations or meet personal goals. But when they hurt one another intentionally, they become locked in a dog-eat-dog struggle that pays absolutely no attention to the relational "us." In each spouse's mind, the only way to survive is to either control or annihilate the partner. Marital survival is most at risk when the relationship is unstable because of the damage it causes to the individual partners.

Marital therapy must always begin by infusing stability into the relationship, for two reasons. First, stability is a prerequisite for trustworthiness, and without trustworthiness, it is impossible for spouses to give to one another. As discussed earlier, in order for relationships to exist, there must be a balance between what partners give to each other for the good of the relationship and what they take for their own needs and nurture. We are driven by this sense of balance and justice to get what we deserve out of the relationship, but in order to earn what we get, we must give. When we trust another, in essence, we commit ourselves to giving to that person without threat or manipulation because we believe that he or she in turn will give us what we need and our sense of balance will be satisfied. When trustworthiness is gone, however, people stop giving and invent ways to protect themselves. This protection is often accomplished by departing from the relationship or taking aggressive and destructive action intended to "make" the other person satisfy the relational needs. In either case, "us" is starved for trustworthiness as both partners move to protect their own interests and cause mutual harm in the process.

Spouses who are unstable hurt one another by inflicting this type of passive neglect or aggressive damage. Instability precludes giving and creates strong individual interests in the face of this loss of trust. In a very real sense, it can do nothing else in relationships. Who would walk out on a ledge on a three-story building with a person who had tried to push us off a few minutes earlier. When we ask patients to communicate, listen, and not try to mind-read another's therapy, we are asking them to trust their spouses. When they have difficulty, we push them out onto the ledge with the very spouses whom they consider untrustworthy. They may go through the motions of acceding to our requests, but they will not trust. It is only when we address the instability directly that we have the opportunity to move spouses into a position to start rebuilding trustworthiness.

The second reason that therapy must begin by dealing with stability in the relationship is related to trustworthiness, but actually is more concerned with power in the relationship. "Us-ness" grows when partners are vested in making their relationship the most powerful influence on their interactions. When there is instability, the spouses start *competing* for the power in the relationship. With both competing for individual power at the expense of the other, the relational "us" is powerless and all but forgotten.

All of us have the power to do good and to do evil, and most of us have done both at various times. When spouses reach a point of instability in their relationship where each strives to garner the power for himself or herself to shape the relationship as he or she wants it to be, they cause interactions at each other's expense, and at the expense of others. This competition for power is evil in that it destroys the relationship. In working toward stability in the marital relationship, the therapist must, at a minimum, be able to move the partners to a place where they will not continue the grab for power. In other words, if the partners are not ready to do good in the relationship, at least they must be stopped from doing harm.

Key Attitudes for Stability

How does therapy affect a particular attitude in patients? Some research suggests that using insight-oriented models to help couples understand themselves and their relationship results in the most long-term stability (Snyder, Willis & Grady-Fletcher, 1991). According to other research, changing a couple's behavior and interactions is the most effective way to produce marital harmony (Jacobson & Addis, 1993). As therapists, we have patients who will do homework assignments, but not be enlightened by their work. They go through the motions but the *meanings* of their actions do not have an impact. Other patients gain insights and new meanings in therapy, but do not put much effort into doing anything different in their lives. As therapists, we can tell when we are really having an effect on our patients' lives when they gain new insights into their lives and problems, and then follow up those insights with actions that change their lives or are aimed at solving their problems. This is when we see a true attitude change in marital therapy when spouses gain insight and find new meaning in themselves and their marriages and then take the action necessary to make the changes in insights we call on them to do.

If changed attitudes in marriage represent changes in *meanings* and *actions*, then good marital therapy approaches are relevant to both insight and behavioral changes. Although the way I choose for a couple to work on their marriage does include both objectives, it is not a set and prescribed pattern. Some couples will work on insight-based meaning and behavioral action intuitively, with little help, instruction, or confrontation on my part. However, when I have spouses who are willing to work only on actions or only on insight, I will usually instruct and then confront.

I have found that there are three key attitudes that spouses need if their relationship is to be stable: commitment to relational preservation, individual humility, and respect for their spouse. I believe that, as a therapist, I should be willing to establish these standards for my patients so that they and I will know what to expect if the marital therapy is successful. Even with spouses who are highly unstable, violent, and destructive, there is almost always the desire on the part of both to do good for each other and the relationship. I believe it is essential that we spell out behavioral and attitudinal expectations, not to shame the spouses for their destructive actions, but to inspire them to meet a higher standard and to illustrate the marital attitudes that most of them so desperately want. Therefore, I try to teach and recall these attitudes again and again when we are working through the issues that cause instability in the marriage.

Commitment to Relational Preservation

Gottman and Gottman (1998) cite research that estimates that a couple will wait six years before seeing help with marital distress. By the time six years have passed, an unstable couple has usually caused enormous damage to both spouses. In essence, the unstable spouses are enemies who do not trust each other, are locked in a competitive power struggle, and, in many cases, do not even like each other. After I watch the partners interact for a while, but still in the evaluation session, I will move them to confront the attitude of commitment to relational preservation. By this, I do not mean that they promise to stay together no matter what happens and that they promise never to divorce. Rather, commitment to relational preservation means that I ask them to stop the damage that they knowingly inflict on each other and the relational "us." The following is from a therapy session with a couple in their early 50s. Each had been married previously, and they had been fighting viciously throughout most of the eight years of their marriage.

Therapist: Medical doctors make a commitment to the idea of "First, do no harm." That means that they are committed to doing nothing to the patient that will make things worse. You two have told me about the struggle that you have been having for many years, and I can see by the way that you interact that you insult each other and are vicious in your yelling and accusations. You both have told me about your reasons for doing this, but now we are entering a new era in your relationship. You have come to marital therapy to see if you can get help. I certainly don't want to do anything that will make your relationship worse, and I want you both to make a commitment to do nothing that will damage the relationship further.

Husband: Like what?

Therapist: Like the insults, yelling, and threatening. I realize that you still have those feelings, but if you act on them, it will make marital therapy difficult.

Husband: We've been at each other so long that it has become second nature to us, a natural response.

Therapist: I realize that, but you are now in a new era. If we are going to be successful in rebuilding or building a good marital relationship, I cannot let you continue to hurt one another. It would be like trying to pour a foundation during an earthquake. I am asking both of you to agree to stop the aggressive retaliatory actions that *you know* will hurt the other. I'm not yet asking you to do anything nice for each other, but I am asking you to do no harm.

Wife: Well, I would be happy to make that commitment if I thought he would keep his end of the bargain. I feel that whatever I do is in response to what he does to me first.

Husband: *(Glaring at the wife)* Oh, right. You never start anything with me, I'm always....

Therapist: *(Forcefully gesturing with his hand)* Stop! You two are now starting to do harm to each other. It will take both of you to make this commitment not to harm one another, but it must start with each of you individually. Just as with this interaction, you must learn to ask yourself, "Is this going to hurt or help?" *(After a pause)* I know that you must want to stop hurting each other and to have a stable relationship.

Wife: Absolutely. That is why we are here. *(Husband nods)*

Therapist: I will help you, but you two must decide whether the time has come to stop hurting each other and to start letting the relationship get better.

Husband: Of course, you are right. That is the reason that we are here. I will make an effort to hold back my anger and not explode.

Wife: I will do the same.

This, of course, is very directive. I chose from the very first session to make clear my intention that, at least in the therapy room, I would not allow damage to be done and instability created. Almost without exception, I can establish this right to stop damage in the first few sessions. This allows me the authority to stop the damage in later sessions when arguments may become more vehement. But it also lets the spouses know that they can join in on the commitment not to do harm. In my experience, most unstable couples are relieved that I broach this subject quickly and are thankful for the boundary of "first, do not harm" to be established. While making this boundary overt certainly does not end the couple's instability and fighting, it does create a safe space in the therapy room, and most couples are able to refrain from doing harm to each other for at least a few days, and up to several weeks.

As a systemic therapist, I believe that the actions of both spouses have caused the marital problems. However, I also know that in highly conflictual situations where instability is high and trust is low, it doesn't take long for one individual to take advantage of another. In asking both spouses to make the commitment to relational preservation, I explain that I am not asking them to let the partner exploit them or abuse them. They must make the commitment together. If one of the spouses is unwilling to make this commitment, I will not ask the other to do so. This is especially important in situations involving violence. In these cases, I seek to create initial stability by establishing stronger individual boundaries, such as leaving, calling for friendly outside assistance, or even calling the police. Boundaries are helpful and absolutely necessary in creating stability, so I am not trying to remove them from therapy. However, therapy can be more constructive if both spouses are willing to move toward doing no harm to the relationship in order to create stability.

Humility

Humility is not a popular word in our culture because we associate it with shame, lack of assertiveness, and co-dependency. We have come to equate humility with the loss of individual pride and self-esteem. No wonder it has become an "dirty word" to the self-help movement!

When I talk about humility, I am not suggesting that couples do better when they are shame-based wimps who believe that they have no individual rights and depend on the marriage for their identity. But I do feel strongly that there is a place for humility in marital therapy. To my mind, by assuming an attitude of *humility*, we recognize that we have *limitations, problems, and inadequacies that can, and should, be improved*. That is not to say that we are not unique, special, and worthy. As I have stated before, I believe that humans are all of these things. But humans are also imperfect. When we deny or gloss over our imperfections in the name of self-esteem or assertiveness, we deny the honesty necessary for self-growth. Carl Rogers, one of the principal gurus of humanistic psychology with its emphasis on self-esteem, valued honesty as one of the main therapeutic components of promoting eventual growth to self-actualization (Rogers, 1961). Part of honesty means that we as individuals are humble enough to recognize our own shortcomings so that we can grow past them.

When we are dealing with an unstable couple, the spouses have usually made an art form of pointing out each other's limitations and problems. They become so involved in looking at the other's inadequacies that they forget to look at their own. In asking the couple to start utilizing the attitude of humility, we are simply asking the partners to recognize who they are and to deal with their own issues. The following is from a therapy session with a couple in their early 20s who had been married for four years. The husband had been spending less and less time with his wife over the course of the marriage and eventually had an affair with a woman coworker. The spouses' interactions had become increasingly conflictual, with the wife accusing the husband of avoidance and the husband accusing the wife of nagging, but the extramarital affair raised the conflict to a new level of damaging statements and accusations. This dialog is from the third session, after much of the anger about the affair and the history of marriage had been revealed.

Therapist: Doing marital work is always tough because you are always having to give up part of yourself to make the "us" relationship work. But what can make it even tougher is that the relationship points out things to you that you really need to change in yourself. For you, Bob, your relationship with Lynn has really pointed up the fact that you are not too comfortable with intimacy and honesty and that you try to escape from conflict. And Lynn, the relationship before the affair was really pointing up how much you depend on Bob for intimacy and how you couldn't think of much of anything else without Bob around. The relationship really pointed out problems, but instead of dealing with the problems, Bob, you ran or stayed away, and Lynn, you got angry because your needs were not being met.

Wife: I know that is true, but I wouldn't have been at him all the time if he had just tried to meet my needs.

Husband: I wouldn't have run away if you hadn't been at me all the time.

Therapist: Certainly, you can point out each other's limitations. The point is, though, that if you concentrate only on your spouse's problems, you won't see your own. Not both of you are responsible for the affair, but both of you are responsible for not looking at your own issues and problems and dealing with them.

Wife: *(After a pause)* That is true. I have known for a long time that I have been desperate in the way I look to him for comfort. I've spent all my time trying to make him different.

Therapist: All that I am asking is that both of you recognize that you have old issues that have influenced you and styles of doing things that are not the best. I want you both to have the humility to recognize that this problem is not all about your spouse; it is about your taking care of some of your own issues.

Husband: I know that I have done that. I've excused myself for doing things I knew were wrong because I would think she deserved it or was driving me away. I've never tried to solve my part in this.

Most couples will readily agree that they are not perfect and that they have individual problems. On occasion, I have had spouses who were so defensive that they could not acknowledge any fault in the relationship. But most individuals will respond positively when I talk about humility and taking their share of the responsibility to do their work.

Humility helps spouses not to think of themselves more highly than they do their spouses. It helps them to be realistic and honest about the limitations, personalities, and characteristics that have shaped their individual personhoods and that need improvement. This prompts spouses to be willing to work on themselves and adds a hopefulness to the relationship. When spouses start looking at themselves, they shift the focus away from their partners. This, in turn, greatly decreases the likelihood that first two "horsemen of the apocalypse," criticism and contempt, will continue in the relationship. Showing the partners that humility is a desirable therapeutic goal helps each of them to deal with his or her own issues that have contributed to the instability and thereby creates more possibility for achieving stability.

Respect

In many ways, respect for the spouse is the opposite of humility. In terms of value, our partners are not any different from ourselves. In other words, they have their limitations, problems, personality issues, and imperfections just like anybody else. But also like us, they are extraordinarily unique, talented, and worthwhile. When we get in touch with our own value without being in touch with our fallibilities, we become arrogant and come to feel that we are beyond correction or reproach. When we realize our value in spite of our limitations, we are humble.

But when we recognize our spouse's limitations without seeing his or her value, we become demeaning and judgmental. We focus on our partner's weaknesses as though we were proving guilt to a jury. We try to make a strong case for his or her shortcomings without leaving anything to chance. We point out every flaw. Worse yet, we fail to see the spouse as a real person who can be hurt by our accusations and attacks. Our spouse is flawed, and somehow we translate that as meaning he or she deserves to treated as junk.

Spouses in unstable relationships are unremitting in their exhibition of this type of judgmental and demeaning behavior. They have lost touch with the other's personhood and have come to believe that each has a right to say or do to each other whatever he or she wishes to say or do. It is only when we see our spouse's value in spite of his or her limitations that we are moved to be respectful of his or her humanness.

When I first bring up the issue of respect in therapy, a typical response of one of the spouses might be, "Respect must be earned," or "I'll treat my partner with respect when he (or she) starts earning it." These statements reflect a belief that our society generally has accepted as a truism. The fact is, however, that humans should be treated with respect just because they are human. No other reason. Humans do not have to earn respect. If I am arrogant enough to believe that I am excused from treating a spouse with respect, then the chances are that I have lost touch with humility. Humility concerning ourselves and respect for our spouses usually go together.

Respect is necessary for a couple in an unstable relationship for two reasons. First, it helps each partner to see the other for *what he or she is*. Our partner is unique and special, but also very fragile, just as we are. We know that we are hurt when we are called disrespectful names, that we feel cheated when we are treated unfairly, and that we see ourselves as worthless when someone demeans or makes fun of our actions. In short, when such things happen to us, we feel abused because our personhood has been dismissed. Our spouses feel the same. They bleed when they are cut and they hurt when they are treated with disrespect.

Second, respect for the spouse helps us to moderate what he or she says to us. Much of the time, what one spouse says to another in terms of complaint or criticism has an element of truth. My wife knows my faults and sometimes states them well, and sometimes does not. If I can excuse myself from hearing her complaint or criticism because I believe she is a "nag" or "so screwed up with her one problems that she has to complain about something," then I do not have to do a thing. The problem remains, however, that I do not grow and I do not work on my own issues. If I do not respect my wife, then I can dismiss what she says about me and not have to change.

Respect helps the unstable couple because it helps the partners to see each other as a fragile, special being who needs nurture instead of attack. It also helps because it allows them to consider each other's complaints and criticisms as material for serious growth work instead of simply dismissing and denying them.

Spouses in unstable relationships, of course, usually do not respect each other and have difficulty imagining how they will ever respect each other again. When I bring this attitude up in therapy, I usually have the spouses associate or recall respect in various ways.

Initial Relationship

Whether it was when the partners first consulted me, when they first dated, or when they married, most couples can remember a time when they respected each other. I often will specifically ask spouses to recall the characteristics they respected the most in the spouse and state them in front of each other. I will then use these statements as the basis for a line of logic that will help reestablish the *grounds* for respect. For instance, the following is from a session with an unstable couple who had been married for 14 years.

Therapist: When you first began the relationship, what were the things that you respected?

Husband: I was attracted to her physically and we had fun together.

Therapist: That's good but that is not quite what I'm asking. I'm asking about the tings that you respected, valued, and thought were special about your wife.

Husband: *(After a pause)* She was supportive and honest. She could always look at a situation, meet it head on, evaluate it, and pick up the pieces.

Therapist: You experience that as encouraging?

Husband: Yeah. When I flunked a course in college, she really helped me do what I needed to do to pass.

Therapist: After these years of marriage, what has made you forget those things that you respected?

Husband: Her negative outlook. She is so anxious about everything and is always imagining the worst.

Therapist: So she is no longer supportive and honest because she is negative and anxious.

Husband: No. *(Pause)* I guess I have forgotten about those things because I'm so frustrated with her.
Therapist: So you still respect her honesty and supportiveness?
Husband: I guess so, yes.

Here, the husband does not immediately feel respect for his wife, but the therapy sets the stage for him to start thinking about attributes that he still respects. Shifting the focus of the spouse can significantly alter the nature of respect between partners and can greatly affect the stability of the marriage. Later in this session, the husband told the wife that although he did have problems with her, he did respect her ability to support and be honest. This, in turn, prompted the wife to name two things she respected about her husband. As a result of their naming the things they had once respected, they were able to have one of their first positive interchanges in weeks.

Recalling What Others Say

If the partners cannot name something they had respected in each other in the past, I will ask them what others respect about their spouses. Often, with volatile couples, if they have any positive attributes to cite, they will quickly discount them by saying that the people who feel that way do not know the "real" spouse as they do. When this happens, I will often use the same type of logic as above, seeking to set the basis for respect. I will ask what the spouse has learned about the partner that destroyed the respect. I then will ask the spouse if those things actually eliminate the respectful things from their spouse's character. The spouse will then recognize that there are things about their partner that are to be respected, but has been ignored out of frustration.

The Universal Belief

In some instances, a spouse will say that there is absolutely nothing about the other that merits respect, either because he or she never deserved it, or once may have, but has now changed. In these situations, I inquire about the person's belief about human beings in general, including himself or herself. I ask, "Do you feel that people are potentially good and can grow? Do you feel that humans intrinsically have value or worth?" Most will respond in a positive way. I then can use this basic belief as a starting point for them to treat the other with at least the minimal respect due him or her just as a human being.

Respect goes a long way toward stabilizing a couple and provides the initial grounds for addressing defensiveness and stonewalling in the marriage. If I respect my spouse, then it is not so easy to attack him or her and not possible to turn him or her "off" as a "nonperson." Also, if I respect my spouse, I am on the road to becoming able to hear his or her complaints about me without moving into a defensive posture.

It is important to state here that with couples who are deep into instability, respect is a difficult attitude to master. If the partners feel individually threatened or are selfish, or if they are arrogant and righteous, respect for the other is hard to achieve. In my experience, respect usually follows the couple's commitment to relational preservation and to each of the partners accepting the idea that he or she has some work to do on himself or herself that will foster humility.

Conclusions

Achieving stability is the first important step in marital therapy because without it, a couple cannot begin to rebuild trust and will continue a destructive effort to gain power. Three important attitudes are necessary in order to build this stability. First, the therapist must move the partners to become committed to the preservations of "us" instead of their individual desires. The relational interest must become the most powerful driving force. Therefore, partners must commit to not intentionally doing harm to the relationship by abusing each other. Second, the therapist must start confronting the spouses about the attitude of humility. This is not intended to demean the partners, but to put them in touch with the important work that each individual must do to improve the status of respect between the spouses. Being respectful is intended to impel the spouses to recognize each other simply as human beings and thereby reduce the tendency to abuse or ignore the other.

I believe that these attitudes should be presented overtly and unequivocally within the first three sessions of therapy. This sets a clear goal of expectations for the couple and allows the therapist to refer them again and again throughout the marital therapy work. In short, these attitudes are essential to stability and are important to the success of work on the couple family-of-origin issues and styles of conflict that so often contribute to instability.

chapter four

Getting the Right Actors on Stage: Family-of-Origin Issues

It is such a classic idea in therapy that we sometimes forget how valid it really is. A man or a woman coming from a damaged relationship with his or her family of origin tries to play out that damage or correct those problems in the marital relationship. It is like that old saying, "Don't try to teach a pig to sing, because you will be disappointed with the results and will annoy the pig." When people try to work out family-of-origin issues with their spouses, the issues do not get worked out and the attempt usually results in harm to the marriage. It is like having the actors for *Romeo and Juliet* on stage and trying to present the play using the script of *Othello*. When this happens, life is being played out with the right actors, but the wrong script.

This scenario can lead to serious instability in a marital relationship. One partner continues to try to get the other partner to fulfill obligations that were unmet in childhood. When the attempt is unsuccessful, the first partner becomes frustrated. As the frustration grows, the other spouse starts to retaliate and their mutual trustworthiness diminishes and the instability escalates. Unless the therapist can help spouses understand their family-of-origin issues and place them where they belong, further instability is the likely result.

It is a difficult thing to accomplish in therapy: Partners come in who have an extremely unstable relationship and usually are on the brink of separating or divorcing. The temptation, as a therapist, is to try to stop the conflict, get some constructive things going in the marriage, and then try to address some of the old family-of-origin issues that undoubtedly are complicating the marriage. I know the frustration also, because there were times when I opted to delay family-of-origin work even though I knew there were serious unsettled issues. But experience is a very good teacher. When I did delay this work, I almost always would find that the conflict would not be stopped, the frustration of the couple wold grow, and we would have to go back and do the family-of-origin work anyway as an entrance into making the relationship more stable. There is no way around facing these issues, when they exist, at the beginning of therapy. If, as therapists, we do not take them into consideration, then we try to meet urgent needs by ignoring the important details and end up not taking care of those urgent needs. I do not believe, however, that family-of-origin therapy must take 18 sessions, or even six. I believe the therapist can gather important family-of-origin information that will *make a difference in the marriage* in two to four sessions. The goal of this work in marital therapy is not to solve all the family-of-origin issues, but rather to clarify them enough to prevent the spouses from poisoning their relationship by pursuing them. The following is a family-of-origin therapy "shorthand": a way to surface the family-of-origin issues quickly so that the spouses can stop them from creating instability in their relationship.

Process of Family-of-Origin Work

In order to do this shorthand, the therapist must know the exact information that is most likely to be played out in the marriage. General questions like, "What can you tell me about the family in which you grew up?" are usually not a productive use of the therapy time. The couple is in trouble and needs help in creating stability. The therapist must learn the vital information quickly in order to use it to help this stability along. I divide the family-of-origin work into three main sources of information I am going to try to identify: the structure and role of the family, the emotional deficits and violations in the family, and any unresolved grief or loyalty issues.

As mentioned before, I try to do the bulk of the family-of-origin work in the second, third, and fourth sessions. Most of the time, I meet with the couple, even though I may be gathering information from just one spouse. I believe that when the spouse hears the account of the partner's family-of-origin from a therapeutic perspective, it helps him or her to understand and appreciate the partner and the relationship. There have been a few times when there was severe violation or abuse in a spouse's background and I met with him or her individually during the family-of-origin session, but this was the exception, and not the rule.

Structure and Role

One of the key complicating factors from a family-of-origin that creates problems for spouses is lack of clarity as to the structure and role of family. It is essential for therapists to remind themselves that patients have no idea of what is normal. Normal is what the patient was exposed to during those formative years. Therefore, what the spouse experienced in his or her family-of-origin will often ordain the habits, expectations, or beliefs that the spouse will bring to the marital relationship. Although these habits, expectations, or beliefs may pose a problem, the spouse will maintain them with very little thought as to their "fit" or "rightness," because he or she is used to them as being the only way of seeing or relating to the world.

I still find it very helpful to recall the old structural family therapy ideas (Minuchin & Fishman, 1981). Central to the idea of structural family therapy is the tenet that the roles, subsystems, and beliefs of the family are dictated by the way that power and boundaries are formed in the relationship. For instance, a man who grew up in a patriarchal family where the father made all the decisions for the family but the mother was the nurturer, as an adult may believe that to assume a man's role, he must have all the decision-making power and must not become involved with child care. He may believe, as well, that real men do not share much with their wives and that being a good father only entails being a good provider. Also, he might separate himself emotionally from the family group to ensure that his wife accepts her role as nurturer, thus leaving her in a coalition with the children. Power and boundaries are formed from the structure of the family.

It becomes the job of the therapist to bring these roles, subsystems, and beliefs to the foreground in such a way that the spouse can understand them and then make appropriate changes where necessary. There are several tools that can facilitate the process of obtaining this information: a questionnaire, a genogram, and belief statements.

Questionnaire

In marital therapy, I find it useful to gather initial information about the family-of-origin through a detailed questionnaire. If I had unlimited time, I might acquire this information through the sessions. However, the press to gain stability in the marital relationship makes gathering the basic information in a written form expedient. There are various forms of questionnaires that can be developed, but the one I use includes some of the following data: (1) Names and ages of parents and siblings and whether the family members are living or dead. This information gives me a head start on constructing a genogram. (2) Occupations of the parents. Many times, the occupations of the parents will give me important leads such as whether the family moved much or whether there was potential family stress. (3) Description of parents. When an adult child describes a parent, he or she is usually giving important descriptors that will indicate whether the parent was emotionally nurturing and fair in his or her treatment of family issues. Also, I find that the descriptions provide some indication of what the spouse believes about gender roles. If it was a bad relationship, the spouse often is groping to make his or her marriage different. If it was a good marriage, the spouse is often using the parents as a definitive model of a good marriage. Also, I find indications in these descriptions of any misuse or triangulation of the adult child into the parental relationship. (4) Descriptions of discipline. The way the adult child was disciplined will give me information about potential abuse in the background. (5) Description of being taught about sexuality. A spouse description of how he or she was given sexual information or learned about the differences between men and women provides important clues as to the openness of communication in the family system. It also can afford insight into any possible abuses in the family. (6) Descriptions of relationships. Often, when spouses describe the relationships in the family, they reveal the emotional tone of the family and whether the family was helpful or hurtful. They usually reveal some of the unmet desires and expectations of what the family should be to them. (7) Any other information. This allows the spouses an opportunity to reveal anything that they feel may help me to understand their backgrounds. Many times, I will learn of traumatic events in the family history, the hope that spouses have for the family, or unresolved grief issues that can complicate a relationship.

Questionnaires do not take the place of therapy, but they do sensitize the therapist to information that needs to be checked out in the session. In addition, the questionnaire prompts the spouses to think about the families from which they came and how those families have shaped important attitudes and roles.

Genogram

A genogram is a family map of the structure of the family-of-origin. McGoldrick and Gerson (1985) suggested a genogram format and how to gather genogram information by first recording names and ages, then by recording coalitions and relationships among family members, and, finally, by recording important events or traumas in the family background. This family map gives both the therapist and the patient a visual history of how the family has affected the individual, in terms of roles taken and of belief systems formed. As such, I find genograms essential.

However, I do not have unlimited time to amass genogram data. I will usually try to do a basic genogram in about 30 minutes of one session. I shortcut the process by first gathering information only about the families in which the patients grew up, as opposed to the three-generation genogram that McGoldrick and Gerson suggest. I do miss details by not utilizing the three-generation complex, but the one-generation genogram usually reveals enough to tell me whether I need to go into it more deeply. In most instances, however, the information on one generation will be sufficient to inform me about any structures or belief systems that are contributing to the instability of the marriage.

I can usually get the bulk of this information from the questionnaire and then confirm the map in the session. I then move to find out the coalitions in the family group. I ask such questions as, "Who was closest to you in your family?" and "What was the relationship like between you and your father?" The responses provide indications as to how boundaries were drawn in the family and whether there was unreasonable enmeshment or disengagement in the family group. Finally, I ask about events that might have shaped the family group and its belief patterns. The following is from a therapy session with a man who acted violently toward his wife and children and constantly berated them. I had just completed drawing up his genogram. His biological father had died when the man was 4 years old and his sister was 2. His mother then married an uncaring man who treated the patient and his sister harshly, while his mother did not defend them.

Therapist: So your mother was essentially more loyal to your stepfather than she was to you?

Husband: I guess so. She didn't have much choice, though. She didn't have the skills she needed to get a job so she really depended on this man to take care of us.

Therapist: How did your mother's choice affect you?

Husband: It ruined my life! *(Laughs)* Seriously, it did make me think that I had to take care of myself.

Therapist: What did it make you feel about the family?

Husband: *(Long pause)* Honestly, it made me feel that you cannot trust anybody. People are just looking out for themselves and they will take advantage of you.

Therapist: So you better look out for yourself?

Husband: So you better look out for yourself because your family certainly won't.

As a result of seeing the genogram, this man was able to identify how his family structure and the trauma related to his father's death had shaped his belief that family members cannot be trusted. When I asked if this were true of his family, the man readily answered that he did not trust his wife and always felt as though she and the children were out to take advantage of him. He said, however, that he had never considered the relationship between how he felt about his present family and the family in which he grew up. The genogram can help to reveal this information quickly and efficiently so that spouses can understand their patterns of interactions.

Belief Statements

As in the case above, belief patterns in the family-of-origin are shaped by the family structure and interactions. However, after I find that the questionnaire or the genogram does not fully reveal these beliefs. Therefore, I make it a practice to ask the patient a series of questions designed to educate the belief patterns that the patient brings to the marriage. The questions are : (1) As a result of growing up in your family, what did you learn about how loveable or important you were? (2) In the family in which you grew up, what was the most important thing to do or be? (3) In your family, how did you know that you were loved? (4) As a result of being in your family, what did you learn was the important thing in family? (5) What did you learn about being or becoming a man/woman from being in your family?

When the spouses answer these questions aloud, it usually marks the first time that they have articulated the way in which their families-of-origin have affected them. I find that when they say these things out loud, they often challenge the logic and belief on the spot and overtly say that they do not want to live that way in their own marriages. At a minimum, it gives me the opportunity to point out how the beliefs, patterns, and roles confuse their marriages and create instability. In this way, I am able to direct the spouses toward keeping their old belief and structure problems in the past and allowing their marriage to forge new patterns and beliefs.

Emotional Deficits and Violations

Many times, with unstable couples, the questionnaire, genogram, and belief statements will reveal that the family-of-origin was particularly damaging to the spouse in question. When people are damaged in their families-of-origin, it is not an intellectual damage that can be corrected cognitively; they are damaged *emotionally* and so are driven to justify their emotional needs. These victims of family damage can carry out very damaging actions themselves, but will not be able to express exactly why they feel compelled to do so.

The model of contextual family therapy (Boszormenyi-Nagy & Krasner, 1980) is absolutely essential for understanding how people are driven by the emotional deficits and violations in their families-of-origins. The idea is that people have an innate sense of justice of what is fair to expect from their families-of-origin. Families should love their members unconditionally and treat them in a trustworthy way. What is trustworthiness for these families? Certainly it entails much, but at a minimum, it would include providing children with care, nurture, discipline, direction, and shelter. The family gives these things without expecting the child to return them. The family's provision of these essentials allows the child to build resources of safety, security, and self-esteem. The child feels loved and supported. From this foundation, the child is eventfully able to engage in friendships, marriage, and parenting and is able to give freely out of his or her resource of love and nurture that was provided by the family. In the trustworthy family, the child does not repay the parents directly for the nurture and care the parents provided. Instead, the adult child passes along the trustworthy resource by giving to the spouse and children that he or she creates. In this way, trustworthiness is passed along in the family-of-origin.

In families that are not trustworthy, however, the situation is very different. In these families, love either is given on condition of behavior or is not given at all. When children from these families have to decide for themselves whether they are loved, precious, unique, and worthy, the decision is clouded by low self-esteem and doubt. A severe violation in and of itself, this is usually coupled with violations of trustworthiness. In these damaging families, the child is not given the care, nurture, discipline, direction, and shelter needed, and in fact, in many cases, will be *required* to provide these very things for their parents. As therapists, we have all seen children who were made responsible for caring for their emotionally needy parents. For example, the 8-year-old who makes dinner for the mother because she is "too tired," or the 10-year-old who listens to and emotionally cares for a father who is lonely and hurt because his wife has left him. These children are pressed into service to give what they should be receiving. It is unfair, but they willingly try to fulfill their family's expectations because they want to be pleasing and to be loved, and this is the only way they know. But a child cannot always fill the adult role of nurturer to the parent's satisfaction. When the child fails, the parent blames the child, which marks the beginning of emotional and physical abuse (Hargrave & Anderson, 1992).

How does this damage the child? From a contextual viewpoint, a child has an innate sense of justice (Boszormenyi-Nagy & Krasner, 1986). When the child does not receive his or her just entitlement from the family-of-origin, he or she does not forget about it as growth occurs. An emotional deficit or violation is created. Instead of having a resource of trustworthiness from which to give to other relationships, the growing child feels compelled to make up for what he or she did not receive.

Unfortunately, this means that the person will feel justified in taking almost any action necessary to secure the nurture and care he or she requires. This, of course, leads to destructive behaviors as the former victims become manipulative, threatening, and abusive in an effort to obtain what they believe is owed to them and see no other way to accomplish it. The destructive actions thus are called **destructive entitlement** (Boszormenyi-Nagy & Krasner, 1986).

Destructive entitlement comes out of the emotional deficits of the family background. Of course, the most likely candidates to be victims of a person's destructive entitlement are the spouse and children. The damaged spouse will know that he or she is being threatening and manipulative, but cannot logically stop himself or herself because the actions *feel justified*. "I was cheated, and this is the only way I can get what I deserve." This kind of destructive action is particularly devastating to the spouse and children because it sets in motion a downward spiral of trust as they move to defend themselves or aggressively become destructive in order to achieve their own entitlement. The result is marital instability.

Spouses are unable to make up to a partner what was lost in childhood. A lover is not equipped to love like a parent. A partner is not meant to love a spouse unconditionally. Trustworthiness between spouses is built by symmetrical give and take, as discussed earlier. Only a parent can provide unconditional love and nurture to a child. When a damaged spouse tried to force his or her partner to give what was lost in childhood, it is pumping in a dry well. If the spouse tries to meet the need, he or she will fail because the effort will neither fill the emotional deficit nor enhance the marital relationship.

So what can be done with these damaged spouses? It is important to remember that the deficit is emotional, and probably has never been articulated in a way that could be understood cognitively. The therapist needs to listen to the story of violation, and then spell out some of the processes that impel the damaged spouse. After the spouse begins to understand the violation and how he or she feels destructively entitled to take inappropriate actions in the marriage, the therapist can help the person keep the problem where it belongs, in the family-of-origin. Often, damaged spouses will want to start individual family-of-origin work in depth to explore how to resolve these issues. I believe that this is appropriate, but not absolutely essential for marital therapy. Most often, the articulation of a violation or deficit adds enough clarity to the situation that the spouse can separate the issues and not expect his or her partner to fulfill unmet needs or entitlements from the family-of-origin. It is best if the damaged partner can accomplish resolution of these violations, but as long as he or she can logically keep the marital and family-of-origin issues separated, marital stability can be achieved.

When there are issues that appear to be violations of love or trust, or of both, I usually find it helpful to work with the damaged spouse utilizing the following exercise. First we talk about the reality that love and trust are obligations of family and that the partner was owed these things in the family-of-origin. Second, we talk about the obligations and entitlements that characterized his or her own family-of-origin. I most times will illustrate this in ledger form (see below) in order to accentuate the fact that the person was cheated out of something to which he or she was entitled and was obliged to give something that he or she should not have been obligated to give. I then can use the questions of the exercise to point out the deficits and violations and how these, in turn, created an emotional drive to be destructive. With this basis, I can direct the person to keep the violations of the family-of-origin out of the marriage or refer him or her for additional family-of-origin work.

❧ *Couple Exercise Two*

Moving Toward Stability
by Resolving Family-of-Origin Issues

Stability in a marriage means that the relationship is a safe, non-threatening, and nondestructive relationship. Above all, it means that the relationship is not harmful.

This makes sense if you are trying to build a loving and trustworthy relationship. If you are consistently worried about or are being victimized by abusive actions, demeaning statements, or neglect, then you cannot build love and trust. Some examples of destructive actions are:

- Use of Physical Force
- Character Attacks
- Demeaning Statements
- Threats of Violence
- Ignoring
- Withdrawing

- Blaming
- Retribution
- Threats of Leaving
- Manipulation

Often, damaging things that we do in a marital relationship are related to the damaging relationships that we experienced in the past. Some of the most important relationships in your emotional formation were the ones in your family-of-origin. How we deal with issues of love and trust were usually taught to us in our families.

Love

Love is a good thing. It teaches us that we are valuable and worthy of care and nurture. What we know about ourselves and our self-images comes from the way we are loved.

Trust

Trust is absolutely essential if we are to experience intimacy in relationships. Trustworthiness is based on our sense of justice. It demands that there must be a balance in what we give to a relationship to keep it going and in what we receive in terms of personal benefit from the relationship. How we act in relationships is usually based on our past experiences and how trustworthy our relationships were.

In the family in which you grew up, you were entitled to be treated in a trustworthy way. List some of the things that you feel you received from your family and the things that you were obligated to give back for the family's good.

ENTITLEMENT (Take) (individual is entitled to)	OBLIGATION (Give) (individual is expected to)

1. Do you feel the ledger is fair? Are there things that violated you as a person?
2. How did the violations damage or hurt you? How does this damage come out now?
3. Are there things that you could do that would help resolve this issue of violation?
4. How can you keep these issues focused on your family-of-origin and out of your marital relationship?

In some situations, the person finds it difficult to articulate the violations in terms of obligations and deserved entitlement. When this is the case, I often find it helpful to examine his or her current behavior. A person who comes from a family with emotional deficits or violations often will internalize the deficit or violation as a way that he or she feels about himself or herself, or a belief as to how he or she needs to act in relationships (Hargrave & Sells, 1997). In situations of severe violations of love, people have a tendency to internalize the lack of love into a (1) rage against the person or persons who did not love adequately or (2) shame resulting from the belief that they were unworthy of love. People who experience extreme rage or shame are usually having difficulty in realizing unconditional love from their families-of-origin. They move into a rage or shame behavior as a defense mechanism in order to deal with this harsh violation. And, as they rage or feel shame, they create instability in their current relationships.

Those who undergo severe violations of trustworthiness view relationships as hurtful. They, therefore, create actions to deal with this hurt (1) by controlling all interactions in the relationship to the point of not being at risk, or (2) by becoming chaotic to the point that they will not be expected them to be responsible in relationships. Controllers call the shots in relationships in order to protect themselves and to look responsible. However, in marriages, they become dictatorial and create instability by making unreasonable demands on the spouse. Chaotic people feel threatened by relationships and try consistently to escape. They will behave irresponsibly.

The result of family violations will be individual pain. As shown in Figure 2.1, the pain is internalized, causing the victim to feel rage or shame and to be either controlling or chaotic in relationships.

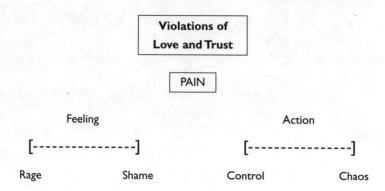

Figure 2.1 Results of Family Violations and Pain

It is often helpful for a person who cannot make sense of violations in his or her family from a ledger perspective to begin by observing his or her own behavior as a result of the violation. In therapy, I will usually lead the person through the following exercise in order to help the person to identify possible behavioral results of the violations. If this is successful, I then find that it is possible for the patient to talk about the violations of love and trust in the family-of-origin more specifically because his or her current violating behavior is usually of the same nature. This affords the patient another way to put words to the violation he or she feels.

◈ Couple Exercise Three

Results of Family Violation and Pain

You are entitled to receive love and trust from your family and it causes deep pain when they aren't provided. If you are like most people, you transform that pain into feelings about yourself (primarily violations of love) and beliefs about actions you must take in future relationships (primarily violations of trust). As the illustration shows, when you are violated, you are likely to feel (1) resulting rage as you experience uncontrolled anger toward your victimizer, or (2) shame as you accuse yourself of being unlovable and not deserving of a trustworthy relationship. Similarly, you are likely to take actions in future relationships that are (1) overcontrolling as you try to minimize your risk of hurt, or (2) chaotic as you assume that little can be done to form trusting relationships and that you will be hurt eventually despite any effort to the contrary.

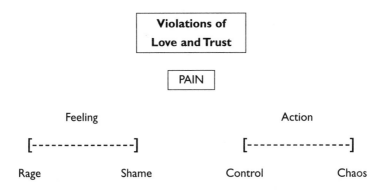

Understanding
Your Style of Dealing with Painful Violations

Directions: Rate the following statements as they apply to you. Since each person is unique, there are no right or wrong answers. Just try to respond as honestly as you can. Please respond to every statement.

After reading each statement, check the answer that BEST describes the way you feel or act.

1. People don't ask my advice or opinion.
   ☐ Yes, I believe this is mostly true.   ☐ No, this is mostly false.

2. Nobody knows how I really feel.
   ☐ Yes, I believe this is mostly true.   ☐ No, I believe this is false.

3. I easily misplace things.
   ☐ Yes, I do this much of the time.   ☐ No, this is rarely the case.

4. I am ashamed of what has happened to me.
   ☐ Yes, I feel this much of the time.   ☐ No, I seldom feel this way.

5. I hit things when I am really angry
   ☐ Yes, this happens often.   ☐ No, this hardly ever happens.

6. Winning is very important to me.
   ☐ Yes, I believe this is mostly true.   ☐ No, I rarely feel this way.

7. I can stay with tasks until they are complete.
   ☐ Yes, I do this much of the time.   ☐ No, this is rarely the case.

8. I need to cover up how I really feel.
   ☐ Yes, I feel this most of the time.   ☐ No, I seldom feel this way.

9. I feel like smashing things.
   ☐ Yes, I feel this way often.   ☐ No, I seldom feel this way.

10. I swear a lot when I am mad.
    ☐ Yes, I do this much of the time.   ☐ No, this hardly ever happens.

11. I don't want people to know what happened to me.
    ☐ Yes, this is mostly true.   ☐ No, this is mostly false.

12. I have difficulty compromising with other people.
    ☐ Yes, I believe this is mostly true.   ☐ No, this is seldom true.

13. I feel hopeless and alone.
    ☐ Yes, this is mostly true.   ☐ No, this is mostly false.

14. It is often better to cover up your feelings.
    ☐ Yes, I believe this is mostly true.   ☐ No, I seldom feel this way.

15. This person causes me to feel so angry, I cannot think.
    ☐ Yes, this happens often.   ☐ No, this seldom happens.

16. I feel responsible for what this person did to me.
    ☐ Yes, I feel this much of the time.   ☐ No, I seldom feel this way.

17. When in an argument, I have been known to throw things.
    ☐ Yes, this happens often.   ☐ No, this hardly ever happens.

18. People say that I'm co-dependent.
    ☐ Yes, I believe this is mostly true.   ☐ No, this does not happen.

19. After work or school, I have no motivation to get anything accomplished.
    ☐ Yes, I believe this is mostly true.   ☐ No, I seldom feel this way.

20. Life feels organized.
    ☐ Yes, I believe this is mostly true.   ☐ No, I seldom feel this way.

21. I feel enraged often.
    ☐ Yes, this happens much of the time.   ☐ No, this seldom happens.

22. People say that I am a person who has to have his or her way.
    ☐ Yes, I believe this is mostly true.   ☐ No, this is mostly false.

Scoring the Scale

The foregoing was taken from the *Pain Scale* of the *Interpersonal Relationship Resolution Scale* (Hargrave & Sells, 1997). The scale is designed to give you an idea of how you deal with violations of love and trust in terms of behavior that can be characterized in the constructs of *shame, rage, control,* and *chaos.*

Shame

Shame is the degree to which an individual internalizes painful or undesirable experiences. Shame is a global measure that assesses the overall manifestation of personal guilt. High scores (10 or above) may mean that the individual is comfortable with mild levels of confrontation and is secure with self. Low scores (8 or below) may indicate that individuals experience excessive guilt and internalize emotions that indicate the self is unacceptable.

Rage

Rage is the degree to which an individual externalizes painful or undesirable experiences. It is a global measure that assesses internal feelings of anger and actions that are manifestations of anger. High scores (10 or above) may indicate that the individual does not express anger in an overt manner. Low scores (9 or below) may indicate that the individual expresses anger and resentment in external ways.

Control

Control is the degree to which an individual seeks to lead his or her life in such a way as to avoid or deal with situations. It is a global measure that assesses overall efforts in managing life. High scores (7 or above) may reflect a relaxed style of conducting activities and relationships. Low scores (6 or below) may reflect an authoritarian style of dealing with life goals or relationships.

Chaos

Chaos is the degree to which an individual seeks to avoid organization or responsibility in dealing with situations. It is a global measure that assesses an overall failure to manage life successfully. High scores (11 or above) may reflect a balanced effort in organizing life goals and being considered responsible. Low scores (9 or below) may reflect an inability to organize and manage life goals and relationships.

Add the following together:

SHAME score

2. I for Yes, 2 for No ____
4. I for Yes, 2 for No ____
8. I for Yes, 2 for No ____
11. I for Yes, 2 for No ____
13. I for Yes, 2 for No ____
16. I for Yes, 2 for No ____

TOTAL: ____

RAGE score

5. I for Yes, 2 for No ____
9. I for Yes, 2 for No ____
10. I for Yes, 2 for No ____
15. I for Yes, 2 for No ____
17. I for Yes, 2 for No ____
21. I for Yes, 2 for No ____

TOTAL: ____

CONTROL score

6. I for Yes, 2 for No ____
12. I for Yes, 2 for No ____

CHAOS score

1. I for Yes, 2 for No ____
3. I for Yes, 2 for No ____

14. I for Yes, 2 for No ____

22. I for Yes, 2 for No ____

TOTAL: ____

7. 2 for Yes, I for No ____

18. I for Yes, 2 for No ____

19. I for Yes, 2 for No ____

20. 2 for Yes, I for No ____

TOTAL: ____

Keeping Pain Where It Belongs

Once you understand your preferred style of dealing with pain, it is helpful to make sure that you keep the pain with the relationships that are responsible for the violation. Too often, spouses who come from families with damaging pasts carry their ways of dealing with pain into the marital relationship. Of course, the problem with this practice is that it is very difficult to live with raging, shaming, controlling or chaotic people, and it usually damages their spouse, their children, or both.

1. What are some examples of violations that you experienced in your family-of-origin or past relationships?
2. Based on the scale and illustration above, what has been your style in dealing with painful relational issues?
3. How might you deal with the painful violations of the past and keep your reactions to that damage focused on the relationship in which they occurred and out of your marital relationship? If you need help, ask a friend or therapist.
4. In the future, how might you avoid hurting your spouse or children when you feel pain?

❧ ❧ ❧

Unresolved Grief and Loyalty Issues

A spouse may have problems in a marital relationship as a result of unresolved grief or unresolved loyalty issues in the family-of-origin. Unresolved grief may be the result of loss through the death of the key member of the family or through a loss of place, status, or relationship. In these cases, the patient's grief causes him or her to make unreasonable or strange demands on the marital relationship, creating instability. This was the case with a woman who had been married for 22 years and who was grieving the loss of her father 25 years earlier, and was turning the grief into anger toward her husband, who was unable to make her feel better.

Therapist: What did your father do for you?
  Wife: He believed in me. He was the only one who made me feel like I could do anything. He made me feel so special.
Therapist: *(Long pause)* Who makes you feel that way now?
  Wife: *(Starts to cry)* No one. There is no one who can take the place of my father. I have felt this emptiness ever since he died. He was all I had.

The woman's grief is clear, but she had never been able to express the grief in a constructive way. Instead, she turned to her husband to fill the gap. The husband, although he tried, was never successful in giving his wife what she had received from her father. Confused by her grief, the woman turned the feeling of grief into anger at her husband for not providing her with the intimacy she needed and deserved. Frustrated, the husband either isolated himself further or berated the wife for her nagging and pessimist. In this case, once the unresolved grief was pointed out, the woman became much less critical of the husband's effort to be intimate as a husband. As the result of continued attempts to resolve and clarify her grief over her father's death, the marital instability was rectified.

Loyalty issues are also at the heart of much marital instability. Most seem to stem from the failure of a husband and wife to relinquish primary loyalty to the family-of-origin in favor of loyalty to the spouse. These issues are usually related to old family roles and structure. In such cases, identifying the structure and existing loyalty issues gives the therapist the opportunity to start setting boundaries between the spouses and their families.

Conclusions

Family-of-origin issues that are carried over into a marriage can act as an unidentified submarine that torpedoes the marital ship. By bringing the structure and roles of the family-of-origin to the surface, identifying emotional deficits and violations, and clarifying unresolved grief and loyalty issues, the therapist can help the partners to do one of two positive things. First, the therapist can assist them in identifying the driving forces from the family-of-origin that create intolerable and unresolvable distractions in the marriage. Second, the therapist can point partners in the direction of how to resolve these family-of-origin issues for their own individual growth and well-being. Achieving these two goals removes the family-of-origin issues as a source of marital instability.

chapter five

Conflict:
Knowing the Pattern of Harm
and Resolution

Conflict in marriage is natural. People do not go about the tough busi-ness of giving up some of themselves for the good of the other and the relational "us" without running into roadblocks along the way. We are built to be relational, but we are still very individually minded. We want our needs, wants, and goals satisfied. Mostly, we think we are right about what we should get, what our spouses need, and how the relation-ship is best served. We are all self-centered at the core. So when we disagree with our spouse, who is also self-centered and believes his or her view right, conflict will be the result.

I am not completely against this self-centered attitude. Individualism serves an essential function in the marriage relationship because it informs the partners of what they deserve to receive in the natural give-and-take of relationship. But it is not difficult to see how, if unchecked, this self-cen-tered attitude can digress into a gargantuan struggle between two egos that are both set on winning. Not all conflict is bad, because inevitably it is the means by which two people work out their individual differences to form the relational environment and personality of "us." But make no mistake, there is bad conflict. Conflict that reaches the point where the partners bru-talize each other emotionally and leave each other empty is bad. It creates a marriage environment where little survives, either as individuals or as "us." It is the type of conflict that, if persistent, creates instability.

The goal of the therapist is not to eliminate conflict from the relationship entirely, but to stop this bad type of conflict from perpetuating damage on the partners and the relational "us." In order to create marital stability, the therapy must help the couple identify how they can work on their differences without harming each other and killing the relationship.

Two Basic Ideas About Conflict

There are two basic ideas that are very helpful to me as I think about conflict in marriage. The first revolves around the idea that conflict is simply a way to work out individual differences and decide the personality of the relational "us." In other words, conflict is part of the relational work of marriage in developing an "us." Mace and Mace (1979) put this well when they spell out three aspects of marital work. First, there are the things that the spouses have in common and on which they agree. These agreements are readily put into the relational "us." Second, there are things on which the spouses disagree and have different preferences, but the two are complementary. For instance, the wife may be very good at organizing their financial records whereas the husband is good at coming up with different ideas on how to earn a larger income. These are very different skills, but the couple could use them both to become a financially successful "us." Finally, there are those things and preferences on which spouses differ and disagree that are not complementary. These are the situations that can become hazardous to a marriage and create instability.

The second basic idea about conflict that is helpful to me is the recognition that couples have different styles of dealing with conflict. As mentioned before, Gottman (1994) identified three styles of conflict or problem solving among couples. The *validating* style refers to spouses who work out their problems calmly and are mutually satisfied with the resolution. In the *conflict-avoiding* style, spouses avoid head-on confrontation and live their lives while disagreeing on various issues. In short, they agree to disagree. However, they seldom achieve resolution of significant details. Finally, the *volatile* couple erupts into passionate and disruptive conflict and resolution of the issues to their satisfaction is rare.

It is important to recall that Gottman reports that no particular style is a guarantee of marital satisfaction or stability, but rather it is the positivity of the marriage as compared with the negativity that is the important factor.

These two ideas are very helpful to me in ascertaining what type of conflict clients are facing. There are spouses who see life very differently from each other and find themselves with material and opinions that are not complementary. With these couples, the potential for conflict is very high. Conversely, spouses who see life in much the same way will have less potential for conflict. For each couple, the style of their conflict is their potential resource in dealing with it. With validating couples, the potential resource is an emphasis on strength and expression. These spouses see each other as equals and have similar opinions on several subjects. That is, they have the potential for producing positives in the marriage, even though their style is no guarantee that they will. On the other hand, those with conflict-avoiding and volatile styles have far less potential for emphasizing positives in the marriage. These styles either avoid interactions that might prove disruptive, or they engage in conflicts that run the risk of overwhelming any positive aspects of the marriage.

When I see a couple and hear stories about the partners' conflicts, I make it a point to try to assess their potential for conflict and their resources for dealing with it. Although we seldom see them in therapy, there are numerous couples who agree on many subjects and perspectives and have good resources for dealing with differences. We do, however, see couples who are what I call midrange couples: they have low potential for conflict, but their style produces fewer positive resources for dealing with any conflict that does ensue. In these instances, although the areas of disagreement are fewer, the couple is unable to deal with those differences easily. Their problems are related to their relational resources. Other midrange couples have high potential for conflict because they have significant differences that are not complementary, but their relational conflict style is much more positive. Although these couples have many disagreements, they are able to bring positive resources to bear to solve them. Finally, there are couples with high potential for conflict because they have an array of differences that are not complementary and they have a conflict style that produces few resources for dealing with the conflicts. These couples have chronic conflicts and are unable to deal with the disagreements constructively. We see many such couples in therapy, and it is spouses like these who undergo the most marital instability.

Marital Violence and Abuse

It is among couples with the greatest potential for conflict and the fewest relational resources that I see the most violence and abuse develop. So when is it just marital conflict and when is it marital violence? Sometimes, it is not as clear as it would seem. Gelles and Cornell (1987) define violence as an act that carries the intention of causing pain or injury to another person. If a person physically assaults another, then it is clearly violence. But what about intimidating behavior, such as assuming a threatening posture? What about throwing things or punching walls? How about name calling or character assassination? In my opinion, all of these qualify as violent behavior. Certainly, we can put these acts on a continuum of most violent to least violent, but I do believe that whenever we become threatening with the intention of intimidating or harming, either emotionally or physically, we are violent.

Marital conflict is ripe for the development of violence when the spouses chronically disagree and express dissatisfaction. Once the conflict turns into contemptuous personal attacks, frustration and aggressiveness escalate. When the escalation begins, spouses who do not have the resources to pull back will become violent.

There are several views of why we are violent. One idea is that the violent abuser is psychologically disordered (O'Leary, 1993) or that the perpetrator of violence is physiologically triggered and aroused to the point of being violent (Jacobson & Gottman, 1998). Another view holds that people learn to be violent by watching violence in their own families and in society at large (Ney, 1992). Still another view posits the idea that since men are the primary perpetrators of violence in the family, violence is a result of the patriarchal social institution that has allowed men to exploit women (Yllo, 1993). In reality, all of these explanations, and others, account for family violence to some degree. From a therapeutic point of view, the important factor to consider seems to be to keep the most damaging conflicts from becoming violent. I personally believe that all violence, no matter where it lies on the continuum, must be stopped. However, I recognize that it is a matter of therapeutic judgment as to when a conflict is just a conflict and when it is violence. In situations where the conflict is violent, there are two broad ideas on how to stop it.

Boundaries

The primary idea behind setting boundaries is to help the couple recognize when the conflict is getting out of hand by being aware of the cycle of violence (Walker, 1979). The first boundary would be set to help the spouses recognize the tension internally and then to disengage voluntarily. If they are unable to disengage voluntarily, then the second boundary would involve one or the other of the spouses' leaving the premises to find friendly support by going to the house of a friend or neighbor. If the violent tension and conflict continue to develop, then the third boundary would be to enlist the support of such agencies as law enforcement or human resources.

Boundaries are necessary but are difficult to establish. However, considering the statistics on violent marriages and the possibility of physical harm to partners, it is essential that the therapist do everything possible to ensure that a couple with a history of violence employ boundaries to keep their conflicts from turning violent.

Compassion and Social Action

Helping a violent person is a matter of individual therapy, not marital therapy. If someone has a history of being violent, simple conflict-resolution skills are not likely to help. Boundaries assist a couple in taking steps to ensure the nonescalation of harm, but the violent person also needs help. Encouraging results have been reported by Steven Stosny (1998), who has developed a compassion model for counseling such persons. His model has shown an 87% success rate with court-ordered batterers. Instead of informing the violent person about the sociological aspects of violence, which tends to shame or blame the perpetrator, the compassion model helps the violent person with emotional regulation. But although this compassion approach makes sense for individual counseling, the therapist also needs to be willing to work on the sociological nature of violence in a more global way. This includes offering classes or sponsoring activities that will promote equality, halting the publicizing of violence by the media, and mobilizing resources to help the victims of violence.

By assisting a couple to create boundaries, motivating social action, and getting a violent person into individual therapy, the therapist is not trying to resolve conflict, but to prevent violence and injury. Violence is a special issue that needs to be dealt with in addition to marital therapy, and is not a subject for marital therapy in and of itself.

Therapeutic Intervention with Unstable Couples

If we determine that a couple is not violent but fits into the category of having high potential conflict with few style resources to cope with the differences, then we have our therapeutic work cut out for us. In my practice, I find that there are two primary ways in which spouses who are locked in conflict that creates instability can be helped to stop the damaging interactions. First, I try to help them recognize differences that are not complementary in a *pattern of interaction and conflict*. I consider this the most effective way by far of helping them expand their resources in order to deal with conflict more effectively. Second, I help the couple to recognize which conflicts are about the relationship and able to be solved versus conflicts that are a result of their own attitudes. I refer to this practice as teaching the couple to *choose the battles wisely*.

Patterns of Interaction and Conflict

How do we become ourselves? It is hard to say exactly. When I was studying undergraduate psychology years ago, the field was leaning heavily toward the idea that social influences in the environment shape human thought, behavior, and personality. We were who we were because of the way we were nurtured. Today, when I teach undergraduate psychology, I note that the field is leaning heavily toward the idea that our genetic heritage has "hard-wired" our thoughts, behavior, and personality. We are who we are because of our basic nature. Even though most people give lip service to the idea that both *nature and nurture* influence our development, each decade and psychological perspective is marked by the tendency to lean one way or the other.

Whatever the reason for our difference—nature, nurture, or a combination of the two—spouses can indeed be very different from each other in how they see life and go about dealing with life issues. Many people take mates who are their exact opposites in various ways. Depending on how many different issues there are and how many resources the couple has, the conflicts that evolve can be severe and create instability in the marriage.

It is the fact that the conflicts are predictable that gives therapists a therapeutic leverage. Most conflicts are not new. Spouses tend to fight over the same issues again and again. They also tend to fight in the same way over and over again. If we can identify the patterns of interaction and conflict that are repeated again and again, we can inform the couple about the touchy areas of their relationship that are at the root of their instability. We can deal with those issues in mediation or therapy, and then enforce strategies for agreement or permanent disagreement. In other words, we seek to settle the issue and set up a point in therapy where the spouses will agree that the issue is behind them. It is rather like the signing of a peace agreement between antagonistic nations. Neither may feel great about the agreement, but it provides a set of rules by which both can live peacefully. Also, if we can identify the patterns of interaction and conflict, we can teach the couple to recognize how the conflict will proceed. This enables therapists to give them early intervention strategies that will stop the sequence of conflict before it begins, or at least before it escalates.

I have developed a list of the polarization tendencies with which I see couples deal on a regular basis. My first effort is to try to identify the area or areas where the couple has the most difficulty.

Need for Intimacy

This is one of the best known and most often observed interactional situations among couples (Guerin, Fay, Burden, & Kautto, 1987). It is based on the idea that some of us need intimacy whereas others are loners. Those with high needs for intimacy tend to *pursue* people in order to meet their intimacy needs. Those who have little need for intimacy tend to *distance* from people in order to meet their needs for separateness.

These different needs for intimacy set the stage for a predictable pattern as the pursuer tries to achieve some emotional closeness in everything from dinner conversations to sex. The distancer, on the other hand, will see the efforts of the pursuer as threatening encroachment on space and privacy. This can lead to conflict escalation as the pursuer criticizes and shows contempt for the distancer, and the distancer either retaliates in fits of anger or responds with defensiveness or stonewalling.

Getting Things Done

This is another well-observed, classic interaction pattern of couples (Guerin, Fay, Burden, & Kautto, 1987). Here, the couple is trying to deal with how things will get done in the marriage. Some of us feel impelled to get jobs and activities organized and accomplished, whereas some feel more comfortable with having others take care of the details. Those with high tendencies to "do" are *overfunctioners*; those with tendencies to let others take care of details are *underfunctioners*.

As one partner overfunctions and struggles to get things done in the marriage, he or she increasingly becomes frustrated by the underfunctioning partner. The overfunctioner comes to see his or her work in the light of, "If it's going to get done, I'm going to have to do it." Underfunctioners can be irresponsible, but often they have a different philosophy of life. The underfunctioner may truly believe that there is reason to relax and not be so aggressive. Underfunctioners may actually pay attention to important things, but may have a different definition of what is important and what is not. Here the conflicts can be particularly nasty as both have ample fuel for criticizing each other concerning responsibility and reliability. The conflict tends to escalate quickly and the long-term interaction breeds hopelessness in the two partners.

Dealing with Change

Olson and DeFrain (1997) identify the basic differences in how people deal with change. Some people hate change whereas others seem to thrive on it. These changes can be as simple as modifying meal menus and schedules or as complicated as reforming the family structure to accommodate adolescent children. Some of us feel as though we need a lot of structure in life and others feel better just "letting things flow." Those who deal with change by relying on strong leadership and rules are more *rigid*. Those who deal with it in a laid-back and passive manner are more *chaotic*.

Those with rigid styles of accommodating change tend to be more traditional and authoritarian. They feel safest when things are predictable and they expend great effort in ensuring predictability. People with chaotic styles thrive on action and see little threat in unpredictability, but feel encumbered by rules. As a result, both become critical and eventually will have contempt for each other.

Problem Solving

Problem solving is related to conflict in that it is often the first attempt to deal with differences. Based on the work of Kilmann and Thomas (1975), some of us try to solve problems by tenaciously seeking solutions while others try to avoid the problems all together. Those who try to solve problems by confrontations and hard work are *aggressive*. Those who try to avoid problems or ignore the issues that cause problems are *avoiding*.

The problem with these two styles are that the persons involved do not cooperate with each other. Both aggressive and avoiding people tend to resent the influence of the other and will try to work without the other. Aggressive people see confrontation as the only way to solve problems, while avoiding people hesitate to take on problems that might solve themselves. Again, both will be critical of each other, but the one with the avoiding style will have a tendency to be defensive through withdrawal or might stonewall the partner.

Dealing with Conflict

Once the initial effort at problem solving fails and the couple engages in conflict, there is a possible polarization in working toward resolution. Satir (1988) identified this well-known pattern of interaction. Some of us want to get problems solved quickly and are very aggressive in demanding resolution to conflict, whereas some are extremely passive when conflicts develop and let others dictate to us where problems exist. Those who are dogmatic and demanding in conflicts are *blamers*, whereas those who allow themselves to be dictated to during conflicts are *placaters*.

Blamers, in general, are usually very volatile in the way they attack a problem and usually end up attacking their spouses. These attacks can be quite demeaning as the blamer seldom takes any responsibility for his or her side of the argument. Placaters, on the other hand, take too much responsibility and frustrate the solution to problems by not demanding that the blamers take their share. Escalation in this style is a result of an asymmetrical pattern in which the blamer behaves more erratically and the placater becomes more overly responsible.

Activity of Intimacy

These styles are modified from Satir's (1988) work, which labeled people as computers and distractors. These modified styles are directed at ways by which we prefer to get intimacy needs fulfilled. Some of us find intimacy most pleasing in the context of activity or directed conversations about activities or opinions. Others find intimacy most pleasing when expressing emotions through verbal or physical means. Those who are more apt to find intimacy in emotions are *feeling* oriented, whereas those who find intimacy in activities are *thinking* oriented

Feelers are likely to label thinkers as mechanical and out of touch. On the other hand, thinkers usually experience feelers as irrelevant or "flaky." Both define the intimate activities that they prefer as being "right," and thus tend to be critical of the desires of the other.

In helping a couple in therapy to resolve the pattern issues, I will have them work through the following exercise. After they identify problem patterns, we will explore arguments and conflicts that they have had in the past or one that is currently taking place. In this way, the spouses are able to step outside themselves and look at the way in which the interactions and the pattern of the conflict take place. I then can suggest new ways to deal with the pattern that will interrupt the escalation of conflict.

I find that once a couple identifies the pattern, no conflict is ever quite the same. If they decide to have the conflict, they usually come back to therapy quite aware of the problems and of the errors they committed. Often, the spouses will see the pattern develop and they both decide to tell what they know about their destructive pattern. Every future conflict, therefore, becomes a lesson on how to get better and better at preventing marital instability. As mentioned before, I believe that this identification of pattern is the single most effective tool available to help the partners stabilize the conflict that gets out of control.

❧ *Couple Exercise Four*

Identifying Your Patterns

One of the primary contributors to instability in the marital relationship is conflict. You have probably heard that conflict in relationships is always inevitable and that you must learn to deal with it constructively. Although it is probably true that all relationships have conflict, that does not mean that all conflict is necessary or profitable.

Most people in relationships develop a style of relating to each other. These styles are sometimes balanced in couples, but often are polarized. When polarization occurs, conflicts are inevitable and difficult to resolve. Here are some common relationship styles. Indicate the ones where there is polarization.

Need for Intimacy

Some of us have a high need for intimacy while others are loners. Those with high needs for intimacy tend to *pursue* people to meet their intimacy needs. Those who have low needs for intimacy tend to *distance* from people in order to meet their need for separateness. Indicate on the continuum where each partner lands.

Distancer [--] Pursuer

Getting Things Done

Some of us feel driven to get jobs and activities organized and accomplished while others feel more comfortable having others take care of the details. Those with high tendencies to "do" are *overfunctioners* while those with tendencies to let others take care of details are *underfunctioners*. Indicate on the continuum where each partner lands.

Overfunctioner [----------------------------] Underfunctioner

Dealing with Change

Some of us feel we need a lot of structure to handle life while others feel better "letting things flow." Those who deal with change by relying on strong leadership and rules are more *rigid*. Those who deal with change in a laid-back and passive manner are more *chaotic*. Indicate on the continuum where each partner lands.

Rigid [---] Chaotic

Problem Solving

Some of us try to solve problems by tenaciously seeking solutions while others try to avoid the problems all together. Those who try to solve problems by confrontations and hard work are *aggressive*. Those who try to avoid problems or to ignore issues that cause problems are *avoiding*. Indicate on the continuum where each partner lands.

Aggressive Style [-----------------------------] Avoiding Style

Dealing with Conflict

Some of us want to get problems solved quickly and are very aggressive in demanding resolution to conflict. Some are extremely passive when conflicts develop and let others dictate to us where problems exist. Those who are dogmatic and demanding in conflicts are *blaming*, while those who allow themselves to be dictated to during conflicts are *placating*. Indicate on the continuum where each partner lands.

Blaming [--] Placating

Activity of Intimacy

Some of us find intimacy most pleasing within the context of activity or directed conversations about activities or opinions. Others find intimacy most pleasing when we are expressing emotions through verbal or physical means. Those who are more apt to find intimacy in emotions are *feeling* oriented, while those who find intimacy in activities are *thinking* oriented. Indicate on the continuum where each partner lands.

Thinking Style [--------------------------------] Feeling Style

Keeping Conflict Constructive

1. What areas are the most polarized and problematic in your relationship?
2. What are some common styles or roles from the list that you employ in dealing with problems in the relationship?
3. How might these roles be avoided in the future?

Choose the Battles Wisely

Much commonsense knowledge, as well as research, suggests that holding back complaints against a spouse and not dealing with conflict are bad for a marriage (Gottman & Gottman, 1998; Crohan, 1992). If we keep things to ourselves, complaints against the other tend to fester. To complicate matters, our spouse most likely will continue to do the very thing that we do not like. The complaint deepens to the point where we criticize, or we separate. It thus makes good sense that having conflict when it is relatively minor has two benefits. First, the conflict is easier to resolve and creates fewer long-term problems. Second, smaller conflicts relieve the pressure we feel to complain to our spouse about things that dissatisfy or bother us. Both of these benefits contribute to the likelihood that we and our spouse will not have a major blowup.

With that said, it is important to note that most spouses hate to fight. Conflict usually produces physiological tension and leaves couples feeling empty inside emotionally. But with couples who undergo consistent and deteriorating conflict that creates marital instability, the situation is much worse. Partners in these unstable couples really are hurting each other with every conflict. Remember the example of the couple in the rowboat, each holding an oar. When the couple is unstable, each conflict is another whack of the oar to the head of each spouse. It hurts the individuals and disables the relational "us."

Therefore, I believe that it is valuable for the marital therapy to train some couples to *avoid* conflict in some circumstances. Please understand, I am not saying that avoidance is sound way to achieve marital harmony. There are conflicts that, while painful at the time, eventually produce good in the relationship. What I am saying is that with unstable couples, most conflict usually results in bad effects on the individuals and the marriage. In addition, some conflict cannot be resolved in the marital relationship.

To my mind, there are three basic reasons why we initiate conflict. The first reason is that we are *egocentric.* In this context, this simply means that I don't like the way you look, act, or think. Most of these issues are focused on our own problems: a desire to exert our power to make our spouse behave or act in a certain way, unacceptance of our spouse, anger over not getting what we want, or the belief that we are superior to our spouse.

The second reason we are willing to initiate conflict is for *retaliation.* I retaliate when something someone has said or done has threatened me. It may be that what he or she has done reminds me of something in the past or a threat to my safety or personal power, but I respond with a defensiveness that either withdraws or attacks the individual's personhood.

The final reason we initiate conflict is that we feel there is an imbalance in the give-and-take relationship. In other words, we sense an injustice between what we receive from the relationship and what we give to it. These issues are brought up because one of the spouses is not doing his or her fair share of the work of emotionally giving and personally contributing to keep the relationship in balance.

It is my feeling that conflicts that are related to egocentrism or retaliation are usually difficult or impossible to "solve" within the context of the relationship. These issues have more to do with individual sensitivity to personal realities. Therefore, there is usually little point to confronting such issues in a conflict. Of course, we are all egocentric and retaliatory at times, and so we will all have conflicts. But there is value in trying to curb conflicts attributable to these two reasons.

In therapy with unstable spouses who are in chronic conflict, I will spell out these reasons for conflict clearly. In each conflict, they have had or are currently having, I ask the couple to identify whether the reason for the conflict has its basis in personal egocentrism, the urge to retaliate, or an imbalance in give-and-take. When they identify the root reason for the fight, they are much more able to back off from fights that cannot be resolved. Again, this technique is designed to help the spouses get outside themselves and analyze the damage they are doing to each other. The following excerpt is from a session with a volatile couple who had been married for six years, and supposedly were arguing about finances.

Husband: *(Very angry)* I don't know how many times I have to listen to you. You are negative about every little aspect of our lives. You make me sick.

Wife: I'm not negative, I'm just trying to protect what we have. If I didn't, you would spend every dime we have made in our business.

Husband: That's not what this is about. It is about your needing to control everything that anybody in the universe does.

Wife: *(Looking shocked)* It is not about me, it is about your damned childishness.

Therapist: Stop. *(Pause)* I really do agree with you that what you have said is not what the conflict is about, but I still don't think you have it. Remember, there are three basic reasons you two quarrel. You either are trying to make it happen your way, are retaliating because you are hurt, or are frustrated because the relationship is currently not fair. *(While the therapist is saying this, he writes the three reasons for the conflict on three separate sheets of paper and places them on the floor. The spouses stare at the written reasons.)* I want to invite both of you to review what you have just said and tell me what the conflict is about. *(Long pause)* Bill?

Husband: I want to be able to say that she is unfair to me, but it really is because I don't like the way she does things. I don't like to be pressed and controlled and I feel that is what she is always doing to me. The reason I'm so angry is that I want it my way.

Therapist: Louise?

Wife: Well, part of this is about what I feel is unfair. I do feel as though he does not take care of our business and it is all piled on me. But I was responding so angrily because he attacked me and I wanted to hurt him back. I was mostly retaliating.

Therapist: Good. So the question now becomes whether you want to pound on each other or you want to solve the problem. Bill, you don't like the way Louise tells you to do things. Is there a way that you could get her to address the problem without trying to make her do it your way?

Husband: I could. But to do it, I would have to watch my thoughts. I am always so ready to pounce on her at the first sign that she is telling me what to do.

Therapist: So you would have to wait and be humble enough to say that you don't have the right to attack her verbally. Also, you would have to respect this fact that she might have a point about you.

Husband: I really don't like to admit it, but that really is true. She is right about me, a little, but not on every point. But I just want to attack her to try and void everything she has said.

Here the husband is analyzing his own reasons for conflict and coming close to the attitudes that will create stability in the marriage—the attitudes of humility and respect. When he works on these attitudes, he is able to move past his reasons for the destructive conflict and move into developing a mind set for a healthier relationship. His movement in this exchange set the stage in the next session for the couple to have a meaningful process session about changing the way each handled the financial arrangements of the marriage.

Conflicts that are brought on by imbalances in give-and-take are valid and need to be worked out in the context of the relationship. However, even if there is good reason for the conflict, the therapist must be cautious not to let the couple fall into a style of relating that becomes destructive. The primary emphasis in assisting the couple to choose the battles wisely is to help each individual to recognize that some conflicts are more about himself or herself instead of the spouse or the relationship. By identifying the reason for the conflict and then pointing the couple back in the direction of humility and respect, the therapist can help them create more stability in the relational "us."

~ *Couple Exercise Five*

Reasons for Conflict

When you find conflict in relationships, a commonsense thought may help you avoid the problem, or at least keep the conflict on track where it can be resolved. Before you engage in the conflict, know the reason that you are going to battle.

There are three basic reasons why we initiate conflict.

Egocentric or Selfish Reasons
These issues are brought up because I just don't like the way you look, act, or think. Most of these issues are focused on my problems of unacceptance of my spouse, my anger, and sometimes the spouse's defensiveness.

Retaliation
These issues are brought up because something you have said or done has threatened me. It may be that what you have done reminds me of something in the past, or is a threat to my safety or personal power, and I respond with defensiveness that punishes by withdrawal or personal attacks.

Imbalance in Give-and-Take of the Relationship
These issues are brought up because one of us is not doing his or her fair share of the work, emotional giving, and personal contributing to keep the relationship in balance.

Conflicts that are attributable to egocentric/selfish or retaliatory reasons are usually difficult or impossible to "solve" within the context of the relationship. These issues have more to do with individual sensitivity in facing personal realities. Therefore, there is usually little point in confronting these issues in a conflict.

1. Think about some conflicts that the two of you have had in the past. Try and classify the reasons for the conflicts. Were the conflicts inspired by egocentrism/selfishness, retaliation, or imbalances in give-and-take?
2. When you feel egocentric/selfish or retaliatory in the relationship, how might you deal with the issues instead of resorting to conflict?

Conclusions

There will be conflicts in every marital relationship, and not all conflicts are bad. However, when spouses have conflicts that consistently result in relational harm or damage, the therapist must intervene to stabilize the marriage. There are two primary ways to interrupt this type of damaging conflict. First, the therapist can point out the patterns of interaction and conflict for the couple. Second, the therapist can help the couple to identify the reasons for conflict. In both cases, the interventions assist the couple in taking a more objective view of the relationship and thereby allow them to make different choices. This not only stabilizes the relationship, but it sets the stage for the spouses being able to relate in a more trustworthy fashion.

Section III

Maintaining a Secure and Trustworthy "Us"

chapter six

Security and Doing
the Work of Marriage

Think back to the couple in the rowboat, sitting side by side, their hands on the oars. When the spouses have achieved stability in the marriage, they have learned to sit beside each other calmly without using the oars to do battle. They have learned to keep their criticisms to a minimum and have, by and large, been able to respect the ways in which their spouses are different, even though they disagree. In short, they are in the boat together and have learned to achieve a sense of safety. However, this does not guarantee that everything is now okay. There are tough waters and other obstacles ahead that will challenge the couple's relational "us." They now have to learn to work together to make sure that the boat can navigate the turbulence and negotiate the obstacles. Their "us" will have to be able to handle financial stresses and strains, child-rearing issues, and balancing the responsibilities for managing their household. Can the "us" handle the challenges or the "work" of marriage?

Doing the work of marriage is what security is all about. Security is the relational attitude that tells the couple that they are in a committed, responsible, and reliable relationship that can meet the challenges of life and survive. Marriage is more than just living under the same roof and being able to refrain from hurting each other. A good marriage includes the ability of the spouses to partner together and to rely on each other. Partners become close to each other because they share the activity that supports familiarity. Security in the marriage relationship builds the spouses' confidence in the reliability of the "us-ness." Security assures partners that there is a predictability to the relationship and that they can count on each other for company on the journey of life.

If a couple cannot do the work of marriage, insecurity will be the result. There are several manifestations of insecurity, but most often what I see in therapy are spouses who function like roommates. Insecurity has bred a mutual feeling of mistrust that the partners cannot be relied on in dealing with leisure, as well as work. Therefore, the "roommates" will divide tasks, with one perhaps taking the responsibility for the children while the other assumes responsibility for the finances. However, this is not a trade-off of responsibilities, but carving out a place for individuality in the marital relationship. As a result, one partner feels threatened when the other takes no interest in his or her assigned activities. The spouses then try to protect themselves from each other and are often dishonest.

The most devastating aspect of insecurity in a relationship, however, is the absence of intimacy. When spouses have no confidence in the relationship, they are indeed alone, and often lonely. This loneliness impels them to seek to get their intimacy needs met elsewhere. If the couple has children, one of the spouses will often turn to a child for emotional support and nurture, and thus become closer to the child than the spouse. If there are no children available, work or career is often the next intimacy substitute. Those who choose this work partnership will know every nuance of their jobs, but their spouses and their home lives will often be a total mystery. Still others will try to fill the loneliness with activity or turn to alcohol or drugs. There are many manifestations of insecurity, but the bottom line is that the spouses do not feel that they can lean into the relationship to do the work of marriage so they lean outwardly and depend on themselves, someone else, or something else to get them through life.

It is indeed hard to stay in a boat if it is not going anywhere. However, the couple is still in that same boat. Even though spouses may carve out individuality in the work of life, there are many aspects of the marriage that affect them both. For instance, the following exchange is from a therapy session with a couple where a husband supposedly was taking care of the finances and kept all details from his wife.

Wife: Some checks were returned to me that I had written on the account. When I called, the bank, they wouldn't give me any information. I thought that was absurd and illegal, so I pressed Jeff about it. Our banker is a friend of his. *(Pause)* Jeff had told him not to tell me anything about our finances, so I started pressing Jeff and threatening him. He finally told me that we owe around $300,000 in personal and business loans. I just went limp.

Therapist: You didn't know?

Wife: No way I knew. I knew that we owed money, but whenever I would try to find out anything about the finances, Jeff would always tell me that he would take care of it and that we were okay. Well the truth is, if I even know the truth yet, that we are not okay.

Husband: We are okay. You know how the business is very volatile and you know that things go up and down very quickly.

Wife: But $300,000? Why didn't you tell me so we could work on this. Instead, last week you bought a new car and let me write bad checks for new furniture.

Husband: I didn't tell you because I knew you would just freak out, like you are doing now. You act a though you didn't have any part in buying and spending. I have kept us afloat up to this point, and I will continue to do so.

Wife: I spent the money because I didn't know.

Husband: Then just let me handle the finances and I will let you know what you can spend and what you can't.

Wife: *(Very angry)* No way. We are not spending money the way you want to and I'm not coming to you for approval.

The couple had acted as if they could go on with their separate goals, but, in fact, the marital finances were a mess. They were still in the same boat. But with the pervasive insecurity produced in the relationship, they were now faced with trying to solve a problem together without trusting each other and with no history of responsible and reliable behavior.

This is the type of marital brouhaha that is brought into the therapy room when the couple's "us" is suffering from insecurity. They have run aground and are not able to do the work of marriage because of the lack of love and trust in the relationship. In some situations, couples who have reached this level of insecurity simply give up on the relationship and divorce. But many times, the insecurity, combined with the stress of life, will prompt the spouses to turn on each other. Such couples often divorce, as well, but not until all the stability in the marriage has been destroyed and both partners have been hurt badly. Achieving a secure relationship, therefore, is a pressing need in therapy. I approach security problems in a relationship by concentrating on building trustworthiness by fostering attitudes of responsibility and reliability.

Key Attitudes for Security

Building security in the "us" relationship is really about building trust. I have discussed the importance of trustworthiness to the relationship previously. When we trust our spouses, we are able to give freely to them and to the relationship because we believe our spouses will responsibly and reliably give to us and the relationship what it and we need. This builds a sense of security and prevents the relationship from drifting into instability. Trust allows us to give because we believe someone will give to us. This kind of trust also allows the relationship to develop a deep intimacy.

Trust allows us to accomplish three key things in relational intimacy (Book, 1980). First, it allows us to count on the fact that our marital relationship will continue. It is the basis for our knowing that we will not be alone and that we can experience the companionate love of another. Second, it allows us to predict how the spouse and the relationship will behave. We cannot live in the past, but past experiences model how we should relate and behave in the future. For instance, if I have been told by my employer that I will be paid at the end of each month and have received my paychecks at the end of the month for years, I can reliably predict that I will continue to be paid at the end of each month and so plan my expenditures accordingly. Partners and relationships have personality and behavioral characteristics that we can predict based on the trustworthiness of the relationship. When I can predict how my spouse and the relational "us" will behave, I can make sure that my behavior will fit the expectations of my spouse, he or she can work to fit with me, and both of us can work for the good of the relational "us." Third, it allows us to know that out of all the relational choices available, as well as opportunities to pursue individual goals, our partner has chosen to be with us. This sets us in a relationship with another person who has willingly chosen to act consistently, and even to sacrifice at times, in order to fit with us. This act of giving for our good raises our self-esteem and contributes to our feelings of worth.

It is fair to say that intimacy exists on three levels (Kieffer, 1977). *Breadth* refers to the number of activities and interests the spouses share. The greater the number of activities and interests, the deeper is the level of intimacy. The second level of intimacy is *depth*. Depth refers to how much commitment and confidence the couple has that the relationship will continue. Depth in intimacy allows partners to see the relational "us" as part of themselves and they experience the marriage and the partner as important to their own feelings of wholeness or completeness. Finally, the third level of intimacy is *openness*. Openness is the comfort we feel in revealing ourselves to our partner through self-disclosure.

Trust serves as the basis of intimacy in that responsible and reliable behavior on the part of the spouses allow them to predict that the other will be committed (depth) and will behave in such a way that each can fit his or her life to the other's (breadth). As this trust grows, they are more and more able to engage in the self-revelation that will result in sincere growth. Therefore, building trust is an absolute essential in the process of developing a growing marital "us-ness." Not only will it afford the couple a feeling of security in doing the work of marriage, but it will put the partners in a position where they can develop a strong, intimate "us."

When a couple is stable, the partners can turn their attention to security issues. Security is a continuing activity, but usually the couple either will achieve security between the second and seventh year of marriage, or will begin to have serious problems. The security issues that I see most in therapy are results of the couple's being unable to work out this important question of trustworthiness in this period of time, and, as a result, they have continued the relationship under untrustworthy circumstances. The deterioration of the trust has resulted in a severe crisis for the couple, usually brought on by irresponsible behavior. The couple has become so unstable that the partners are blaming each other for the "problems" in the marriage. Security issues are usually very specific, such as complaints about money, work, or parenting, and each generally will require from one to three therapy sessions to be dealt with successfully. Building trustworthiness encompasses two key attitudes that must be developed by the spouses: *responsibility* and *reliability*.

Responsibility

It is hard to underemphasize the importance of responsibility in maintaining relationships. When the couples I see are having marital troubles, one of the spouses will often say, "I just don't love him (or her) anymore." When I explore the issue further, I usually find that it is not a question of love, but a loss of *trust* in the other. Nothing kills a relationship more quickly and makes spouses angrier than having their partners deny any responsibility for contributing to the relationship.

What is responsible behavior in a relationship? It varies from marriage to marriage, but I would maintain that couples and therapists know it when they see it. Most of the time, it is obvious, as when spouses cannot depend on each other to maintain a steady job or get the bills paid. It often centers around one spouse's not taking enough responsibility, or taking too much, in caring for and raising the children. Many times, it includes an imbalance in the activities that keep a family going. Specifics may vary, but the imbalances are evident. What, for me as a therapist, is really the telling sign when I see an irresponsible couple, is the spouse who wants the partner to do something for him or her that he or she is not willing to do for the other. The spouse might as well say, "I don't care about fairness. I want to take advantage of your giving to me and I don't want to give anything in return." Spouses will invent manipulative or threatening excuses to maintain such logic, but the irresponsibility is still clear.

When working on the issue of responsibility, I will often give couples the following exercise. I know, and will explain to the couple, that the basis of trustworthiness in a relationship is responsible giving. What we give should be in balance with what we receive. When there is an imbalance between what an individual receives and the obligations he or she fulfills, trust will deteriorate. Often, spouses will know intuitively that things are imbalanced. However, in situations where the couple may have difficulty in coming to terms with the unfairness of the relationship, illustrating the interaction on the ledger below is helpful. In order to use this ledger, however, the couple must be directed to focus on a particular issue, such as parenting or housework.

❧ *Couple Exercise Six*

What Is Your Relational Ledger Like?

After a relationship is somewhat stable and safe, it is time to make it grow and flourish. Most would agree that they don't just want a relationship that won't damage them, but one that is intimate. Intimacy is wonderful. It reveals yourself to your spouse in such a way that you not only feel closer to him or her, but you learn to know yourself a little better. Intimacy in relationships brings people closer together and usually leads them to grow as individuals.

But in order to achieve intimacy, you need to be able to trust your relational partner. Remember, trust is absolutely essential if we are to experience intimacy in relationships. Trustworthiness is based on our sense of justice. It demands that there be a balance between what we give to a relationship to keep it going and what we receive from the relationship in terms of personal benefit.

This is not complicated; it simply means that in any relationship, there is a ledger. On one side of the ledger are things that I'm entitled to *take* from the relationship. On the other side of the ledger are the things that I am obligated to *give* to keep the relationship going.

Balanced Give-and-Take

The give-and-take in a relationship should be balanced in such a way as to uphold our sense of justice or fairness. As we interact with spouses, we are interdependent. This requires us to assume responsibility for our actions, accept the consequences of how we carry out a relationship, and strive for fairness and balance in the relationship's give-and-take.

If we can say that relationships rely on a balance of obligation (give) and entitlement (take), we can illustrate them by setting them up like a bookkeeping account. The left side of the ledger account would represent the (take) that I am entitled to receive from my partner: respect, care, and spousal intimacy. I am entitled to these things partly because that is what husbands and wives provide in our society, but mostly because I am expected, or obligated, to give those same things to my spouse that he or she is expected, or obligated, to give to me. On the right side of the ledger, my obligations (give) that maintain the relationship are listed. Here you find the same obligation to my spouse that I am entitled to receive. The relationship is balanced, symmetrical, and fair, as we give to each other.

For example:

ENTITLEMENT (Take) (individual is entitled to)	OBLIGATION (Give) (individual is expected to)
1. Respect	1. Respect
2. Care	2. Care
3. Intimacy	3. Intimacy

Building Trust

When we have this type of balance between giving what the relationship requires and receiving that to which we are entitled, then the sense of fairness is satisfied. As this balance between give and take continues, we experience trustworthiness in each other. As we experience trust, we are enabled to give to the other. In other words, as I do my part in my relationship with my spouse and he or she does his or her part, I give freely because I trust that he or she will give me what I need. I do not have to threaten or manipulate to get it. When my trust level is high, I work on fulfilling my obligations, confident that my just entitlement will be fulfilled.

When relationships are put into this context of fairness regarding give-and-take, we can understand the function of human emotions. Emotions are simple barometers or gauges that give us a reading on the status of balance between relational give and take. When we do not receive what we deserve, we become angry. On the other hand, when we are overly compensated by a relationship to which we have not contributed, we may feel guilty. The balance of give and take in any relationship includes the emotional field of both the individual and family relationships.

Trustworthiness either is accrued or depleted in relationships. Going back to my example in Chapter 1, say my wife wanted to go away for a few months to write a novel. She would be entirely removed from the family and certainly would not be contributing her fair share to the relationship. The burden of care for the family and responsibility would fall on me. However, since we have had many years of balanced and fair relating, I would agree that my wife should go because I believe that she would do the same for me if I were to make such a request. I would have a large reserve of trust that would enable the relationship to continue as it was, even though it would be unbalanced for several months. I fulfill the extra obligation because I trust that my wife would do the same for me if our roles were reversed. However, if the reserve of trust between the two of us had not been built, it would be unlikely that I would willingly agree to her going.

Trust, however, is never a static resource. Just because I trust my wife today and have enough trust in reserve to accept her not contributing to the relationship for a while does not mean that it will never be a problem. For instance, if after three months of working on her book, she were to ask for another three months, I might agree, but not be so amenable to the idea. If, at the end of that time, she were to refuse to come home, I might find my trust resource depleted because of the extended period of living in an imbalance of give and take. I would feel denied my entitlement from the relationship and probably be unwilling to give freely. I might make some threats or be manipulative in order to get my wife to come home. Trust is built by balanced and fair relationships and is depleted when relationships are imbalanced. Even the best of relationships are endangered when trust is gone.

You may not know all the specifics of the ledger, but overall you know when you are giving more than you are receiving, and vice versa. When I am underbenefited by the relationship, I feel cheated, and *you are not trustworthy*. When I am overbenefited in the relationship, I feel guilty, and *I am not trustworthy*.

When either or both of us are not trustworthy, the relationship is not trustworthy. We feel *insecure* and that puts us into a mentality where we feel as though we are in a "grocery store during a hurricane." We feel threatened, so we go on a threatening, manipulative binge to get everything we need at our partner's expense. When we do this, more damage occurs, trust deteriorates, and the relationship worsens.

1. Using the above ideas, list some of the things that you think would be fair to put in a relational ledger with your spouse.

ENTITLEMENT	OBLIGATION
(Take)	(Give)
(individual is entitled to)	*(individual is expected to)*

2. What is the current status of the relational ledger? Are you or your relational partner being cheated? (Note that you can ask yourself how you are feeling emotionally toward the relationship to give yourself direction. If you feel angry and cheated, chances are that you are not receiving your entitlement. If you feel guilty and manipulative, chances are that you are not fulfilling your obligations.)
3. How much trust is there in the relationship?
4. What changes would have to be made in the relationship to get back to the place where there was a balance and trust was being built?

Responsibility is such an essential element in answering the question of how we should act because, when we are recipients of responsible giving, *we know that the relationship will continue and we will have our needs met.* We will not be taken advantage of and we can be confident that our needs will be met. Someone else is looking out for us and that person believes it is his or her responsibility to meet our needs. This factor is primary in enabling us to consider our spouse and fulfill our responsibility instead of only thinking about ourselves.

Reliability

Whereas responsibility is believing that it is my obligation to meet my spouse's needs, reliability is the discipline and consistency required actually to meet those needs. Many people feel responsible for doing their parts in their marriages, but are so undisciplined or so inconsistent in actually acting that their spouses do not trust them at all. Consider the repentant alcoholic, agreeing with his or her spouse that he or she needs to take responsibility for getting help and meeting his or her obligations, only to be drinking again the next week. When giving is not reliable, trustworthiness is impossible to build.

When people are recipients of reliable giving, however, they know that they can depend on their spouses. They have had clear demonstrations that their spouses will come through again and again. When the spouses fail to meet their obligations, as everyone does occasionally, they are able to compare the spouse's inactions with the overwhelming evidence of reliability. People do not need a perfect spouse, but they do need a 90% reliability rate. When they know that their spouses are reliable, *they can be hopeful* about the future.

In therapy, the attitude of consistency must be constructed by self-reference. I have found that most spouses who are inconsistent do not believe themselves to be so. In other words, they believe that their consistency is consistent enough to engender trust, or they have ample excuses to justify the inconsistency. Often, when this pattern develops, it represents an imbalance of trustworthiness in the person's family-of-origin. If I have not already done so, I will ask questions about the person's history in detail and do some family-of-origin work. However, in any event, I must move the person to confront the inconsistency by directing him or her to the expectations that he or she would have of a relationship. This was the case with a man who was unreliable in many areas, but was currently discussing the issue of parenting with his wife. They had been married for 14 years and had a 9-year-old son and a 7-year-old daughter. Both husband and wife had jobs that required them to work some 40 hours a week. The husband did have family-of-origin issues that resulted in passivity in his relationships, and which were discussed in an earlier session.

Husband: I am a good father. You don't give me any credit.

Wife: I am telling you constantly about how I need help. It is not enough for you just to check out the kids when you get home. I need you to take an interest in their lives. When they do something wrong right in front of you, you don't say a word to them, but wait for me to do it. You don't help them with anything and you don't help me to get them ready for school or bed.

Husband: I help with those things, you know I do.

Therapist: *(Getting the husband's attention)* You help with those things? Tell me about the ways you help your children and help your wife with your children.

Husband: I occasionally give them a bath or put them to bed. If they bring something to me for which they need help, I help them.

Therapist: How often does that happen?

Husband: Probably a couple of times a week.

Therapist: I am not trying to detract from what you do with your kids, but how much attention do you think your kids need?

Husband: They do okay. I know that I could always do better, but I feel I have a good relationship with the kids. I do what I can.

Therapist: *(To the wife)* If you were to do the same amount of parenting as your husband, how much time would you spend with your children?

Wife: I guess a couple of times a week, like he said.

Therapist: *(To the husband)* What would be the result if your wife were to spend only as much time parenting as you do?

Husband: *(Pause)* I guess there would not be much parenting.

Therapist: What would be the result for your kids?

Husband: It wouldn't be good for them.

Therapist: I'm not trying to minimize what you do for your kids, but it sounds to me as though you agree that if your kids just got as much parenting as currently comes from you, it would not be enough and they would suffer. Parenting is a job that is tough enough to do right when we know how difficult it is and spend a lot of time on it. But it is impossible to do right when we delude ourselves into thinking that what we do is okay and spend no time at all. *(Pause)* You want to be a good father who can be counted on, right?

Husband: Of course.

Therapist: If you were one of your kids, would you see yourself as a good father who could be counted on to take care of you?

Husband: No. I had a father like me.

Therapist: Then it is time for us to confront your inconsistency and identify ways in which you can become a more reliable parent.

Husband: I agree.

Confronting unreliability is very difficult therapeutic work. In the above case, as in most cases, both spouses are irresponsible and unreliable in working together. It is important to balance confrontation on issues between the spouses so that one partner does not feel the prime subject of the therapy. But confrontation is necessary in helping patients become more responsible and reliable in their marriages. Confrontation, however, does not have to be angry and shaming. It works best when the patient is forced into the position of confronting himself or herself. In the case above, the man's self-referencing what it would be like to have himself as a father helped him to confront his own inadequacy as a parent. Once this denial is confronted, the therapist can work with the spouse to identify responsible behavior and consistent actions that he or she should try to attain.

A spouse often will be irresponsible or unreliable because he or she believes that the partner will pick up the slack. This can occur when the untrustworthy spouse is an *underfunctioner* and is married to an *overfunctioner*. In such cases, trust deteriorates, but one spouse takes care of the responsibilities of both, so the bills are paid on time, jobs are kept, and the household continues to function. Another therapeutic method for helping spouses confront this type of irresponsibility and unreliability is to set up ways for the untrustworthy spouse to experience the consequences of his or her behavior. In many situations, just exposing the consequences and beginning to draw the necessary boundaries will encourage the spouse to become more reliable and responsible. The consequences of one's behavior are a very effective teacher in real life, and we can also utilize the lesson effectively in therapy.

Conclusions

It is trustworthiness that inspires individuals to function well in relationships. Love tells us who we are and trust tells us how we are to act. But it is not only how we trust each other that lets us know how we should act individually, trust also defines how the relationship will act.

"Us" is like a child that both spouses have created. It will define its identity by how it is loved and will develop a style of acting based on the trust with which it is treated.

In order for "us" to grow and be intimate, it must be characterized by security. Security in marriage is built when the spouses see it as their responsibility to give what their partners and their relationship need and then give those things consistently in a reliable way. When marriages are secure, they have a resource of trustworthiness that will allow the partners to face life together and hold on to each other in good times and bad.

chapter seven

Men and Women Are from Earth: Work and Power in Marriage

It is a difficult for a modern therapist to take a position of anything resembling moral responsibility. The cultural belief system, the confusion over "truth," even the training of psychotherapists, emphasize moral neutrality (Doherty, 1996). Everybody seems to be peddling some type of "truth" or "rightness," whether via religious rigidity or relative redefinition. What or whom are we to believe? Is it not better just to agree that everyone has a point and, although we cannot know which points are valid, generally accept their positions and points?

Like Doherty (1996), I believe that we, as therapists, no longer can enjoy the luxury of not taking moral positions because of the eventuality of damage to moral responsibility. I would readily acknowledge that there are many things that we cannot know. I would further acknowledge that in those instances where we do not know, we should hold our positions tentatively and welcome and accept debate as we learn from other people's positions. But the fact that we do not know everything does not mean that we do not know some things. As I have stated before, I believe that we have an innate sense of balance between what we owe to a relationship to keep it functioning and what we are entitled to receive from the relationship. We have a sense of justice. This sense of justice requires the concept of balance and ability to recognize the fact that we are sometimes out of balance. Injustice occurs when someone is not doing his or her part in a relationship. Injustice occurs when someone is not assuming his or her *responsibility* to give.

If security and trustworthiness in relationships depend on this responsible and reliable giving by partners, then irresponsibility and unreliability destroy relationships. This is where the "rub" for therapists becomes a reality. If we say that there is no "truth" or "right" in terms of actions and behaviors, and that we all are entitled to our own beliefs, then there is little reason to hold on to relational justice. When we, as therapists, see hurtful actions in relationships, it is our sense of justice that is being attacked. It is telling us that the action is unfair, or, in fact, wrong. We may not know everything, but we do know when people are damaging each other and acting irresponsibly. If we hold to the reality that there is relational injustice, then we must deal with the reality that there is relational responsibility. If people are responsible for their actions, then there are things that are "fair," "true," "right," or whatever word we choose to use.

What I am saying is that we see things in relationships that damage the partners individually and damage their relational "us-ness." I cannot take the position that if an action is not good for one but is good for another, then I cannot take sides. For instance, if a husband has an affair with another woman and leaves his wife and family, I cannot see it as morally neutral or "okay" just because the husband would be hurt if he stayed and the wife would be hurt if he left. Although it is true that they may have competing individual interests in the husband's staying or leaving, the relationship's interest, the good of "us," is being destroyed. I see it as part of our responsibilities as therapists to try to be more informed, not less informed, about moral injustice and irresponsibility. We not only should be agents of justice looking out for individuals, but we also have the moral responsibility to look out for the good of "us" relationships. When one individual damages another, we should be willing to admit that the damage was done. Likewise, when someone damages the relationship between himself or herself and another person, we should be willing to acknowledge the injustice and take a stand for responsible behavior. We cannot know everything that is "just" or "right" in relationships, but we do know something.

Security in relationships relates to how the couple builds trustworthiness in handling the work of marriage. When one of the spouses does not do his or her part or does it in an unreliable way, it is up to us as therapists to promote greater responsibility and reliability. Therefore, I take positions that I hope will foster individual responsibility in the marital relationship. I do not do this because I believe that I am "right," but because I know that for the marital relationship to be secure, partners must adhere to a balanced give-and-take in order to build trust.

One of the more insecure areas of today's marriages is the subject of work. Work, as I use the term here, means the work that provides the income necessary for the family to survive and the work that accomplishes the everyday functional and emotional tasks that allow the family to function. Formerly, the assignment of work in a marriage had been strictly a matter of gender. However, the last century has seen tremendous changes in the traditional gender-mandated roles, and those changes have forced us to confront the issue of justice and trustworthiness in marriage. Many of the problems that are brought into the therapy room have at their roots injustices related to how men and women view their contributions to the family and how they meet the family's expectations. This chapter is designed to help couples deal with these changes and be morally responsible in deciding on the division of work in the marriage.

Societal Shifts

Patriarchy, Radical Deconstructionism, Gender, and Work

Men and women certainly differ in terms of physical strength and aggression (Saxton, 1993), which may account for the development of patriarchy. In the hunting-and-gathering, male-dominated societies of the ancient past, the job of the men, with their superior strength, was to search for food, while the role of the women was to raise the children and to gather sustenance when the men were unsuccessful (Gough, 1971). In the later agricultural societies, patriarchy flourished. Men could now own property and the accumulation of land and livestock was a primary symbol of male power. Children were valuable as inexpensive labor in those societies and so the women were expected, or forced, to bear many offspring and to care for them. Women had no choice but to depend on the men and they were relegated to work that would be compatible with

child rearing. This developed a set pattern that continued into this coun-
ty's agrarian past and women become tied more and more to household
chores and child rearing and men became responsible for the outside
work and had all the decision-making power in the family (Margolis,
1984). With the industrial revolution, families began increasingly to
move from rural, self-sustaining settings to urban employment environ-
ments. Men maintained property and decision rights, and continued to
dominate the women, whose role decreased even further in value. The
work that women had performed in a rural setting was not as needed in
an urban environment, and neither was the labor pool of children.
Women and children became more of an economic liability than the asset
they had been on the farm (Saxton, 1993).

Women started moving into the workforce in the late 19th century,
working as unskilled laborers until the 1920s, when there began to be a
demand for semiskilled office personnel. By the mid-1930s and 1940s,
women were joining the labor force in significant numbers, spurred on
during World War II by the need to cover the "home front" while the men
were serving in the armed forces. This ability to earn their own wages
prompted the first social change in the family regarding the status of
women by giving them the opportunity to enjoy single life away from their
families-of-origin before they married. In addition, with the ratification of
the 19th Amendment giving women the right to vote, they were able to
gain some behavioral freedom from old social mores (Hargrave &
Anderson, 1992). Then, in the 1960s, the advent of the birth control pill
as a popular and effective contraceptive allowed women to control the
number of children produced, thus providing them with a way to plan
their education and career and to make family choices (Fathalla, 1992).
Indeed, since 1960, birth rates have declined dramatically (Exter, 1991),
and now some 70% of women work outside the home (Saxton, 1993),
and more women than ever delay marriage, remain alone and never marry,
or maintain the status of single head of the household (Fuchs, 1988).

One of the problems that came with this shift in the status of women
is that marriages were not, and still have not been, modified to accommodate the change. This is certainly true on a societal level, but nowhere
does it show up more clearly than around the issue of work. Not only are
married women working outside the home, but they have been steadily
increasing the number of hours they work, giving them less discretionary
time (Fuchs, 1988). It should be noted here that over the same period,

husbands have decreased their total number of hours worked. So women do more of the work to produce income to help the family to survive and men do less than they did before. In return, do men offer a trade-off and take more of the responsibility for keeping the family functioning physically and emotionally?

The answer is No. Hochschild (1989) revealed disturbing trends in two-income families. She discovered that the women in these marriages, in addition to their jobs, do most of the household tasks, such as cleaning, cooking, taking care of the children, and assuming the responsibility for seeing that the home is well maintained. Men, on the other hand, prefer to do such work as home repair, car maintenance, or lawn care, and feel little responsibility for helping with the household chores. If men do perform these activities, they are likely to frame their work as "helping" with functions that belong to the wife. As a result, women spend an extra four and a half months, 40 hours a week, on household work than do men. There is little wonder that working wives and mothers are more likely than any other group to experience anxiety, depression, and feelings of apprehension (Thoits, 1992). This fact that women provide more of the work needed to produce the family income but men do not provide more of the work needed to help the family function is devastating to justice in the marriage. I can think of no other single cause of the fact that marriages have become more unstable over the last 15 years. How are these structures and practices maintained?

There is no doubt but that the tradition of patriarchy has been a primary contributor. The patriarchal bigotry that spawns the belief that women are either genetically or socially inferior to men and so should be relegated to the roles specified by men is damaging not only to women, but also to the "us" relationship of marriage. In the face of this unfairness, a radical deconstructionism has developed. Radical deconstructionism, as I define it, is the belief that the old power structures have failed and so must be reconstructed to provide opportunities for power to groups that were previously denied it. Although certainly not all feminism is a corollary of radical deconstructionism, there are radical feminists who insist that the only way to reverse patriarchal bigotry is for the men to be deprived of their power and for women to dominate the social structure. The problem, of course, is that this type of structure would cause the same type of damage to individuals and relationships as does patriarchy. The fact that society still treats men as superior to women has not been reversed by the legislative actions of the last 30 years, despite the efforts of the radical deconstructionist movement or radical feminists.

This is where the concept of "us" is very helpful. Men and women are different in a variety of physical, mental, and emotional ways, but both have equal responsibility for "us-ness." They both share the responsibility for deciding how the *relationship* will accomplish the work of marriage. So differences between men and women are not as important as how the individuals come together to accomplish the work. For the "us" marriages to be secure, they need a model of fairness that is equitable and workable.

Traditional Versus Egalitarian Marriage

One of the concepts that has evolved in the study of marriage and the family is that of traditional and companionate marriages. Traditional marriages are those in which there is an emphasis on prescribed roles for each spouse. Men traditionally have been the breadwinners, sexual aggressors, and decision makers. Women traditionally have been the nurturers, caregivers, cooks, and maids (Sperry & Carlson, 1991). In other words, in traditional marriages, the man's role as income provider would take precedence over any efforts to keep the household functioning, whereas the woman's work to acquire income would take second place to her household duties (Blair, 1993). Egalitarian marriages, on the other hand, would tend to deemphasize the definition of roles in favor of shared responsibility for both types of work.

Both traditional and egalitarian marriages, however, pose difficulties. Traditional marriages are unfair by nature because the power for decision making is vested in the man, and have become even more unfair as a result of the increasing participation of women in the paid workforce. Egalitarian marriages would seem to be fair, but, unfortunately, they do not work well in reality. For one thing, it would be difficult for both partners in the marriage to share every task equally. But the primary reason they do not work is that there are admitted differences between men and women. For example, there are stereotypical, but mostly true, differences in the ways that men and women communicate (Tannen, 1990), as well as differences in how they solve problems and provide nurturing. Thus, sharing tasks equally only tends to frustrate both men and women.

One alternative to the egalitarian marriage is the companionate marriage. In companionate marriages there are no prescribed roles, nor is there any attempt to divide every task equally. The "work" of the marriage is decided through negotiation and choice. There is no set standard of *quid pro quo* that dictates equality; rather, the couple senses a way of dividing the work, and of offering trade-offs, that is equitable.

Companionate marriages are a logical solution for several reasons. First, the work in these marriages is fairly divided, and this builds trustworthiness and security. Second, they do not require the spouses to get into battles over absolute equality, but allows them to have a natural "feel" for balance in the relationship that fits with reality. Finally, this type of marriage is good for both the man and the woman in that it accommodates neither the dictates of patriarchy nor the overreaction of radical deconstructionism. For these reasons, I take a strong position with regard to work and marriage. When spouses present to therapy because of some work issue, I usually try to help them move toward a companionate, equitable marriage. To do otherwise maintains patriarchy and eventually will lead to more marital insecurity.

Therapy with Issues of Work and Gender

It can be easy for therapists to ignore how inequity in the work to keep the household functional can affect a marriage. Therapists tend to treat these inequities by teaching the couple active listening techniques or communication exercises. As mentioned previously, the accumulated stress of working to provide income without the help of the husband in accomplishing household tasks takes a physiological toll on the woman. And the fact that the inequity persists sets the stage for deepening the wife's resentment of an uncooperative husband (Hochschild, 1989), which, in turn increases insecurity and prepares the way for conflict, and perhaps the dissolution of the marriage. While I do believe that communication concerning these issues is important, I consider it more important—and indeed essential—for the therapist to help the couple move toward an equitable balance of work.

Men and Trash

My wife, Sharon, is a marriage and family therapist. She says that she hears a complaint so often from women that she is going to write a book about it. The complaint always starts with a sentence something like, "The only thing that I ask him to do is to take out the trash, and he won't even do that one little thing." Men and trash is a common subject in therapy, but it is usually brought up by women who have become so resentful of, and frustrated with, the inequity in the work to maintain the household that they can stand it no longer without demanding redress.

It is probably difficult for men to understand the enormity of their irresponsibility in this area. Most did not grow up in homes where the equitable sharing of household tasks was modeled. In addition to this lack of modeling, many men have been influenced by a patriarchal society that has taught them that it is okay for them not to do their fair share. When dealing with these issues with men in therapy, I try to point out the issue of equity, but also the issue of a male resource for the family. In the following case example, the 44-year-old husband was in therapy because his wife, age 45, had filed for divorce. The wife had stated clearly in the first session that she was divorcing him because she was already caring for three children under the age of 12 and she did not need to care for a 45-year-old.

> Wife: I have tried to reason with you but you will not listen. You never do what you say you will and you never help me. I have to provide all the care for the kids. I do all the laundry. I cook the meals and do the cleaning.
>
> Husband: I do those things when you ask me to.
>
> Wife: *(Glaring)* When I ask.... When I ask you do those things. You have eyes, you can see the that work needs to be done. But unless you have specific instructions from me, you come in and sit on your butt and do nothing!
>
> Husband: Well excuse me for earning a living. You don't know what it's like. I come home and I have to unwind.
>
> Wife: You forget that I work, too. When do I unwind? I don't. I'm working all the time anyway, so I might as well do it without you.

Therapist: *(To the wife)* Let me try to help a bit. I know that there are several areas that you are upset about, but can we start with one specific area that you want to be fair? It can be big or small.

Wife: *(Thinks for a moment)* I don't know. I guess cleaning the house.

Therapist: Good. *(To the husband)* How much housework do you normally do in comparison with your wife?

Husband: Well compared with her, not much. But she is a neatnik. She always wants everything perfect! *(The woman gets angry, but the therapist stops her from saying anything)*

Therapist: She may be neat and you may like things messy. But there are some things that have to be done in a house to keep it clean and safe. Would you agree?

Husband: Yes.

Therapist: Good. So of those things needed to keep the house clean and safe, how much do you do as compared with your wife.

Husband: Not much.

Therapist: How much? Do you do 20% compared with her 80%?

Husband: Probably something like that.

Therapist: Now I know you do other things. How would you justify doing only 20% of the housework when your wife also works outside the home and she does 80%.

Husband: I do work hard, but she'll probably say that she does too.

Therapist: Does she?

Husband: Yeah. The real truth is that I just don't think about those things a lot of the time. I don't even want to think about them.

Therapist: I can understand. But here are some things that I want you to think about. When you don't think about doing your fair share of the work, your wife has to do a little more of your job. It's like a coworker at your job giving you his or her work. That would make you angry, and it makes your wife angry. My wife and I have a saying, "There is not man's work and woman's work—there is just work, and there is too much of it." If you do not do the work, it will overwhelm your wife like she is saying that it already has, and I suspect

that it will continue to make you feel guilty. She will feel
cheated to the point where she will move ahead with her
plans to divorce you.

Husband: So what should I do?

Therapist: Your fair share.

At this point, the husband expressed a willingness to do his "fair
share." When it comes to imbalances and injustices regarding work, I
choose to detail the work that is to take place, for two reasons. First, men
who have never done household tasks need specifics to let them know
what is expected and what to do. Second, it clearly outlines the tasks so
that we can specify the division of labor and the trade-offs that will be
equitable. This is essential because it helps women with the concept of
equity so they can now count the activity as an effort toward building
trust.

I usually use the following exercise to get these specifics down on
paper. Under the headings "Husband" and "Wife" utilitarian function
and intrinsic function are listed. Utilitarian functions are such activities
as cooking, cleaning, and yardwork. Intrinsic functions are emotional
activities like nurturing, talking, and taking time to be with someone.
Work to accomplish household tasks, such as home care and child rearing, includes both utilitarian and intrinsic functions. In the case here, the
household work was a utilitarian function. I will usually use this exercise with a variety of subjects, utilitarian and intrinsic, until the spouses
are able to do the exercise themselves. For instance, the spouses in question were given five exercise sheets: house cleaning, cooking, car
pooling, helping the children with their homework, and putting the children to bed.

❧ *Couple Exercise Seven*

The Work of Marriage

There are basically three types of marriage.

Traditional Marriages
These are marriages that have traditional role structures where the man is responsible for being the breadwinner, financial planner, decision maker, and home repairer, while the woman is responsible for acting as nurturer, house cleaner, child-care provider, and cook.

Egalitarian Marriages
In these marriages, all tasks are divided equally between men and women. Even though the result is equality between men and women, it can be cumbersome for them to do all tasks together; also one spouse may be better than the other at completing a task.

Companionate Marriages
In these marriages, the work is divided in a trade-off fashion so that men and women can do the tasks that they are best at completing and share the work that is unpleasant. Even though in these marriages the work is not divided exactly equally, there is a sense of equity because of the trade-off of tasks.

What type of marriage best fits the relationship at the present time?

All marriages must accomplish work to keep the household functioning. This includes utilitarian functions, such as housework, yardwork, child care, bill paying, and maintenance. It also includes intrinsic functions, such as emotional nurturing and fun activities. In traditional marriages, the man sometimes will take over more utilitarian functions in exchange for the woman's providing more intrinsic functions. When this trade-off is imbalanced, problems will result. In egalitarian marriages, men and women should share utilitarian and intrinsic functions equally, but the balance is hard to maintain. In companionate marriages, men and women divide the labor and trade off the jobs at which they are more likely to succeed, but the trade-off is equitable.

Below, choose a task or set of tasks (such as housework, cooking, home repair) and list the utilitarian or intrinsic functions regarding that task performed by the husband and wife.

Activity or Task: _____

Husband		Wife	
Utilitarian	Intrinsic	Utilitarian	Intrinsic

1. Generally speaking, is the breakdown of function balanced? If not, where are the imbalances?
2. If there are imbalances, what are the things that each partner could do to correct the imbalance?

It is not always the man who is guilty of not doing his fair share of the household work, but that is the case most of the time. In those instances where the women are not maintaining the balance, the same exercise can be used. But in any case, when a partner is not doing his or her part, it is not only the guilty party who maintains these imbalances. The spouses (mostly women) are victims of the same patriarchal thinking that has so often influenced men. Many times, when negotiating tasks in the relationship, women will seek to maintain responsibility for accomplishing certain tasks because they feel that it is their "job" or they fear the consequences if they don't. This is a legitimate position in some cases, but in most situations, it is necessary for the women to "resign" from the responsibility that they have been shouldering unfairly in the relationship. For instance, in the foregoing example, we began negotiating some of the cleaning chores in a trade-off to make the division of work more equitable. The wife needed help in backing off from "her" responsibility to ensure that the husband would take his responsibility.

Therapist:	So there are two bathrooms. What do you want to do here?
Husband:	Well, it would make sense for each of us to clean one.
Wife:	*(Rolls her eyes)* I don't think you will clean a bathroom. I'll always have to check it.
Therapist:	So you don't think he is capable of cleaning a bathroom?
Wife:	Oh, he's capable. I just know that he either will not do it or will do a superficial job. I'll always have to check.
Therapist:	*(To the husband)* Can you figure out how to really clean a bathroom? I mean really make sure that the tub is scrubbed, the toilet is clean, corners are taken care off, mirrors are shiny...can you learn to do that?
Husband:	I know how to clean.
Therapist:	*(To the wife)* If he knows how to clean, then there is nothing for you to do but give him time to see if he will take the responsibility and reliably do his part. If you are always checking, you will still be in the position of being a mother of the bathroom, always seeing if it is done right. Either he will do it or he won't do it, but if you both agree to this division, he will be responsible. You can judge whether he has done his part, but you can't be responsible for the bathroom anymore. So I guess I'm asking you to resign from this responsibility so that he will have to take it.
Wife:	Will he do it?
Therapist:	You have to resign first, then you can see whether he does his part. You will know whether he has or he hasn't.
Wife:	You're right. I'll back off.

When a relationship is insecure because of an imbalance in the division of work, there are few things that a therapist can do that are more effective than sending the underperforming spouse home to do housework. When men do household chores, their wives respond to them better and become more trusting of the relationship. Their stress lessens. Moreover, men who do housework are healthier physiologically and are better able to deal with conflict and emotional intimacy with their spouses (Gottman, 1991). Intervening in the work of marriage not only is justified, but it makes a difference in the security of the marriage.

Power

It is not just housework, however, where there are imbalances that destroy security in marriage. The process by which decisions are made concerning work is a difficult issue for both men and women. Here, the effects of patriarchy and radical deconstructionism have been equally damaging to marriage. Men have been taught to dominate with regard to decision making. They exert this power in overt ways, such as telling women that their views do not matter, and also in covert ways, such as withdrawing from discussions or taking actions without first discussing them with their wives. On the other hand, many women have been taught never to accept being dominated by a man and so may act in a similar manner toward their male counterparts.

As in negotiating utilitarian and intrinsic tasks, decision making in marriage must be equitable. It is acceptable for one or the other to assume the decision-making authority if both partners agree and the responsibility for making decisions is at least partially divided. However, if one partner has total decision-making power, it is likely to result in exploitation of the other. This imbalance contributes to the instability of the marriage.

The effects of societal issues, such as patriarchy, or reaction movements, such as radical deconstructionism, are difficult to reverse in therapy, but the therapist must be willing to confront these problems because of the harm they can inflict on the relational "us." I will use the following exercise to try to bring these power issues to the surface and direct the couple toward a more companionate and secure relationship.

❧ *Couple Exercise Eight*

Power In Marriage

Perhaps no other societal issue has arisen in the last century that has caused so much conflict in relationships than the changing roles of women and the resulting "gender wars." Consider just a few of the changes:

- We have changed from a predominately rural to an urban society. This has provided many more opportunities for women and role flexibility.
- Most married women work outside the home.
- Effective birth-control methods have made it possible for women to do family planning.
- More women than men are college graduates.

These and other changes have made it possible for women, and some men, to attain enough power to press the point that has always been true: women are equal to men. This truth, however, has not been universally accepted. Two factors work against that acceptance:

Patriarchal Bigotry
This is the belief that women are either genetically or socially inferior to men and so should be relegated to certain roles that are specified by men.

Radical Deconstructionism
This is the belief that the old power structures have failed and must be reconstructed to provide opportunities for power to groups that did not have power in the old structure.

An approach that does make sense is intelligent feminism, which promotes equality of power and responsibility between men and women and works against both extreme positions—patriarchal bigotry and radical deconstructionism.

When it comes to marriage, gender roles have been characterized as traditional, egalitarian, and companionate. Traditional roles usually mean that men are to be the "breadwinners" while women are to be "nurturers." Egalitarian roles mean that men and women may interchange or perform the same roles in the relationship. Companionate relationships seek to divide work and to trade off roles and the decision-making power so that the relationship is *fair*. In a companionate relationship, the trade-off of working for money versus home care and nurturing between the man and the woman must be somewhat equal. Power in decision making must be shared.

Power in Marriage

This almost always includes the ability to make decisions in the marriage and then carry them out. There is little support or logic to maintain any position except that men and women should share this power *equally*.

1. Generally speaking, who is the more powerful in the relationship? (Who "gets his or her way" or who "makes things happen" most often?)
2. Is the person who is more powerful in the relationship using patriarchy or radical deconstructionism thinking to maintain his or her role?
3. What would be a more justified power arrangement in the relationship?
4. What are some beliefs about men and women that you will have to give up in order to have a fair relationship?

Conclusions

Working in therapy to attain trustworthy relationships means that the relationships must be based on a balanced, or justified, give-and-take. This fact demands that the therapist take a position on the question of moral justice to help spouses achieve responsibility for what they should do in their marriages. This particularly applies to the inequities between the man and woman in a marriage in terms of how they divide the work that provides income and the work that accomplishes household tasks. In addition, the therapy must address the issues of decision making and power in the relationship. In all of these areas, the therapy must help the relational partners take responsibility for contributing their fair share in order to maintain equity and achieve stability in the relationship.

chapter eight

Taking Care of Business: Money and Marriage

Our interactions in society are driven by money in that we cannot get the goods or services we need, obtain the enjoyment or entertainment we want, or fulfill our obligations without it. Like it or not, money is essential to our well-being. Therefore, how we handle money in marriage becomes part of the well-being of the relational "us" well-being. Therapists have been aware of the interplay between finances and our degree of satisfaction for many years (Poduska, 1993). Money problems are consistently among the top four reasons that first-time marriages end in divorce and are the primary reason for remarriages (Albrecht, Bahr, & Goodman, 1983). Further, spouses who have financial problems do not get along as well as those who are problem-free, and experience more psychological and physiological stress (Voydanoff, 1991)

Part of the real work of marriage, in terms both of providing income and of performing household tasks, obviously involves the acquisition, use, and management of money. Spouses who work together in trustworthy ways in handling financial stress do so by sharing roles, practicing joint decision making, and giving the wife greater influence and making the husband less dominant (Schaninger & Buss, 1986). However, if they cannot work together here, then the likelihood that the relationship will face problems of insecurity is enormous. I find that money issues among couples are seldom about the money itself. There are spouses who have very little money but have strong, stable, and secure marriages, just as there are well-to-do couples with great marriages, but as therapists, we see couples from every part of the economic spectrum— poor, middle income, and wealthy—who are out of control financially and insecure in the marriage because of the stress of money problems. Therefore, in order to help these couples, I believe it is necessary to ascertain the meaning of money to the partners, how they use their money, and what coping skills they have utilized to handle their financial difficulties.

Therapy Issues with Money

The Meaning of Money

Since money is so essential to one's well-being, it is a very powerful factor in life. Although we can conceptualize the power of money in several ways, for me it is most helpful to think of it as a threat to one's well-being. This is true whether one is poor or wealthy. Physically, money has the power to be a threat because if I do not have it, I cannot acquire the goods and services that I need. My current financial situation may be satisfactory but the loss of a job or a downturn in the market can rob me of the capability to meet my physical demands. Emotionally, money is associated with influence and success. It is difficult for a person with very little money to get feedback that will build self esteem. On the other hand, for a person who does have money, there is always a drive to attain even more so that one will be perceived as even more powerful and more successful. Again, the threat of losing one's money brings with it the threat of losing one's power and self-esteem.

Thus, money is a powerful threat in terms of both physical and emotional potential harm. Most of us grew up in families-of-origin, particularly in Western cultures, where this threat was a constant fear. How we saw our families deal with the threat by and large determined how we developed our own attitudes toward money. All of these attitudes are dominated by the fear of the threat, but some of us handle the threat better than do others. In my opinion, the reactions to this fear can be plotted along a continuum. At one end of the continuum would be those who handle the potential threat that money poses by overindulging. At the other extreme would be people who handle the threat by underindulging.

Overindulging

Overindulging is a way of dealing with the fear of losing money by basically saying that you try to get all the money you can and then spend it to satisfy needs and desires. In other words, you will use money to make yourself happy so you will not have to deal with the threat that money poses. The problem, of course, is that you will always have more and more "needs" (better food, a better car, a better place to live), so you will always be in need of more money. At the root of overindulgence is a basic irresponsibility that adheres to the philosophy, "Eat, drink, and be merry for tomorrow we die."

It is not difficult to find support for overindulgence. Consumerism in most Western cultures produces an environment that endorses the idea that we "deserve" to have more and better things. We associate this accumulation of things with happiness, and so have come to use overindulging as a cure to for our emotional ills. This, of course, results in the irresponsible assumption of debt burdens, which, in turn, reduce flexibility and freedom. If overindulgers are responsible enough to settle their debts, then they pay a high price in emotional stress and having to work longer and harder. But, if they are irresponsible, they eventually will try to escape the debt by declaring bankruptcy or going further into debt. Of course, capitalistic societies support the notion of debt, and so it is easy for individual overindulgers to comfort themselves with the thought that "everyone is in debt up to their ears," and so excuse their own irresponsibility.

Underindulging

Underindulging is a way of handling the fear of money by trying to control our finances so that we can "guarantee" ourselves that we will always have enough. The problem with underindulging in order to establish this guarantee is that you can never be sure that something won't happen that will deprive you of your "safety net." If you have enough savings to last six months, what if you lose your job and are unemployed for a year? If you have a million dollars, you can be sued and lose it all in the legal proceedings. Underindulgers respond to the threat of money by hoarding and stockpiling financial assets. Whether rich or poor, they deal with the threat of money in the same way.

One of the difficulties with underindulging is the fact that many underindulgers appear to be very responsible. Who could argue that it is not wise to save for the future and plan for catastrophe? In reality, however, underindulging is just as irresponsible as overindulging. In the dogged pursuit of controlling the fear of physical and emotional harm, underindulgers will often irresponsibly deny themselves or others basic necessities, reasonable enjoyment, or logical uses of their resources.

Both overindulging and underindulging can become habitual in that the chaotic or controlling behavior becomes a dominant force in life. For instance, I have known overindulgers who claimed not to be able to get through a day without wanting to buy something. This was the case with this man, who was discussing a purchase of a sailboat.

Wife: He purchased a sailboat last week. Honest to God, a sailboat. We haven't even been to a lake since we were married.

Husband: I wanted something that we could use to relax. I figured that this would be a good opportunity for all of us to spend time together.

Wife: *(Shaking her head)* You know what kind of financial mess that we are in. How could you think we could even begin to pay for a boat?

Husband: Hell, I don't know. I just know that we don't have very much pleasure in life. We always seem to manage somehow and I just feel like we deserve some things that would help us enjoy life.

Therapist: Do you often find that purchases make you feel better? That you are getting more of what you deserve?

Husband: All the time. If I feel a little down, buying something diverts my attention.

Therapist: How often do you feel down.

Husband: *(Laughs)* Almost every day.

On the other hand, I have know underindulgers who were so caught up in the behavior that they refused to buy basic hygiene products for themselves or would plan all their meals using nonperishable food so that they would not have to have a refrigerator. Such was the case with a woman who was complaining that her husband's behavior was becoming unreasonable.

Wife: He has lost it. I came home last week and my refrigerator was gone. In its place was one of these little refrigerators you find in an office or dorm room.

Husband: We didn't use it that much anyway. The stuff that we buy is
           mostly nonperishable. Besides, the small one uses a lot less
           electricity.
Therapist: And why would you want to get rid of the refrigerator in the
           first place?
Husband: To save money. If we don't have the space, we won't buy as
           much. And it does save on electricity.
Therapist: And why is it so important to save money? Can you not man-
           age financially?
Husband: We are okay, but we can always do better.

The extremes of overindulging and underindulging are in response to
the same fears, but are worked out very differently. The responsible use
of money, of course, lies in a balance of overindulging and underindulging. Money, whether we don't have enough or we lose what we
have, poses a significant threat. It is a requirement of life that individuals
learn to manage their resources responsibly so that they will have enough
to meet their physiological needs, now and for the foreseeable future. At
the same time, however, there is no way that individuals can totally iso-
late themselves from the risk associated with having two little—or too
much—money. Again, a balance between overindulging and underindulging behavior is the key response to the threatened risk.

In working with couples with financial issues, I first will try to help
them deal with this threat of money by identifying their coping strategies—whether overindulgent, underindulgent, or balanced. I then will use
the following exercise to have the spouses talk about some of the issues
that might explain the causes of their behavior and then help them to
identify alternative behaviors that are more functional and adaptable.

❧ Couple Exercise Nine

Understanding Motivations in Using Money

Financial issues are one of the primary ways by which couples promote
insecurity in their relationships. Generally, there are two major problems
when couples contribute to lack of trust and insecurity in handling money.

Overindulging

Consumerism is rampant in most Western societies. We have come to believe that we deserve more and more things and experiences. We have come to believe that these things and experiences are absolutely necessary to our happiness. We have "bought in" to these ideas so much that when we are unhappy or slightly depressed, we use spending to meet some of our emotional needs.

As a result, we often get into a habit of spending without limits. This creates debt burdens and eventually leads to a fear of not being able to meet our basic needs. In addition, it reduces our flexibility and free time to the point where our lives basically are devoted to work to pay off the debt.

Underindulging

Many of us have experienced the fear or reality of not being able to fulfill our basic needs. Often, in response to this fear, we try to compensate for the riskiness of life by hoarding or stockpiling financial assets. As a result, we will often deny ourselves or others reasonable enjoyment and the logical use of those resources.

Either extreme of behavior can be destructive to a relationship. Often, people in a relationship will have an attitude that sanctions overindulgence for themselves, but underindulgence for their spouses. This "turnstile" behavior is hard to cope with because of the double standard it represents.

1. Indicate on the continuum where you and your partner land in terms of overindulgence or underindulgence.

Overindulgence [----------------------------------] Underindulgence

2. How is money currently used in the relationship? (Is it used to ensure happiness or to cover fear?)
3. In the family in which you grew up, was there more overindulgent or underindulgent behavior? How has that affected your attitude toward money?
4. If there is a problem with the use of money, is it primarily overindulgence, underindulgence, or both? (Be sure to be responsible in the way you answer; don't make excuses!)

5. What are some ways that you could begin to be more responsible and reliable with regard to money matters? How do you intend to make it happen?

Using Money

Whether spouses are overindulgers, balanced, or underindulgers, they come together to *use* money in their "us" relationship. Each may have a basic drive to deal with the fears that money poses, but the two will have to determine the use of money together. Arond and Pauker (1987) identified four basic orientations with regard to the use of money: as status, as security, as enjoyment, and as control.

Money as Status

Money is used as a symbol of power and success. The more money or material goods accumulated, the more the perception exists that the couple or individual is powerful or successful.

Money as Security

Money is used as a means of protection. Potential fears or problems are dealt with by financial resources as a barrier to the risks of everyday life.

Money as Enjoyment

Money is used to achieve satisfaction. Money is seen as a resource to be spent on activities or goods that provide a sense of satisfaction and happiness, whether for oneself or others.

Money as Control

Money is used as a means of maintaining independence. Preventing the individual or couple from becoming dependent on family or friends is a primary motivation.

Of course, none of these orientations are wrong in and of themselves. Most would agree that one should use financial resources to achieve a sense of success and well-being, security, enjoyment, and control over one's own destiny. However, problems arise when spouses differ on how to use money or when they become extreme in any one orientation. For instance, the following couple was having difficulty in dealing with their differences regarding money. The man was 53 and the woman was 52. Both of their children were in college.

Husband: You tell me where the money is going to come from. We have two kids in college, we are facing retirement in 10 years, and you don't work.

Wife: I know you work hard to make sure we have enough. But I also know that we have plenty of money in our savings account. I want to use some of that money for things to make our life better. I'm not talking about frivolous things. I want to redo the kitchen and for us to go on a vacation together once a year. I don't want to spend everything, I just want to spend some of what we have.

Husband: If we spend it, we never will get it back. Then what happens if I lose my job or become disabled?

Wife: We can't plan for everything.

Although the wife was somewhat balanced in terms of being overindulgent/underindulgent, the husband was a confirmed underindulger. He was motivated to use money as a means of providing security and control, which is very common among underindulgers. The wife, who wanted to use the money for a little enjoyment, was put into a position of feeling hopeless. Any comment about spending some of their resources would be met by the husband with harsh criticism. As a result, the woman withdrew more and more and began to create her own bank account so that she might use money for her own projects. This infuriated the husband, as he believed that she should use any resources she accumulated to ensure greater family security.

When spouses are at odds over how to use money, it creates an atmosphere of distrust that eats away at the couple's security. If the issue is left unaddressed, they begin to take individual actions motivated away from the relationship that appear to be irresponsible to the other spouse. When this is the result, the therapist must assist the couple in finding a balanced way to use money that is both responsible and reliable. For instance, in the case above, the therapist suggested a middle ground where the spouse could work out of the fears and hopelessness that each other's actions produced.

Therapist: Both of you have a point about the money. I always feel that a balanced view of money means that you have enough to feel as though you are getting somewhere, you have enough to feel safe, you have enough to enjoy, and you have enough to take care of yourself. The problem is that you *(the husband)* concentrate on the part that deals with feeling safe and taking care of the family while you *(the wife)* only talk about what you want to enjoy.

Husband: I only talk about it because we really aren't safe. We are always one step away from financial disaster.

Therapist: I do not doubt you. How much money would make you feel safe?

Husband: What do you mean?

Therapist: How much money would make you feel safe and secure so that you would feel comfortable with spending some of it for enjoyment?

Husband: Comfortable enough to spend it? I don't think I have ever been comfortable spending.

Therapist: And that is my point. As we identified last week, you have a tendency to handle your financial fear by underindulging. Although it is understandable considering your background, it closes out the possibility of using resources to enjoy life. If you were single, that might be an option. But you are in a relationship that requires that both of you give some so that it is not just one way or the other.

Wife: I don't want to spend all of our money or savings.

Therapist: I really do believe you. But because your husband is an underindulger, he never hears you. All he hears you talk about is how you want to spend the money and he doesn't hear enough of your concern, as well, about keeping the family safe and secure.

Wife: I do want us to be safe.

Therapist: How could you *(the husband)* be assured that she is concerned about the family's security?

Husband: If she would also contribute to our savings and stop pressur-
ing me about spending the money.

Therapist: Well, that would do things the way you would want them
done. But how would you also move toward using the money
for things you would enjoy?

Husband: *(Pause)* I know that she deserves a new kitchen and I know it
needs to be redone. It just feels unsafe to me to spend the
money.

Therapist: I understand, but if you are asking your wife to set aside
some of her priorities for the good of the family, shouldn't
you be willing to do the same?

Husband: If we are going to be okay, I've got to give a little.

Therapist: You have to give, so that the relationship will be better. I can
help talk you through your fear, but you need to be responsible to the relationship.

Husband: I can give that a try.

Some couples will agree on the use of money, but will be so badly out
of balance that they become irresponsible. Such was the case with a husband and wife who were spending money to achieve status and to enjoy
themselves and becoming more and more financially irresponsible.

Wife: We are thinking about buying a new house in The Meadows
(a particularly exclusive area).

Therapist: *(Pause)* Considering your financial problems, that comes as a
surprise.

Husband: We have just been thinking that we are going to be dealing
with this financial stress for a long time and eventually may
have to declare bankruptcy, so we might as well be in a place
where we are both happy.

Wife: We found someone who will lend us the money, although it
will be at a higher rate because of our past problems.

Therapist: Who decided to buy the house?

Husband: It was my idea.

Therapist: *(To the wife)* Did you think it was a good idea?

Wife: No, but the more he talked about it, the more I could see that
he really wanted this to happen. It does make sense.

Therapist: Any reservations?

Wife: Plenty.

Husband: You said you felt okay about it.

Wife: I do, I do.

Therapist: The question is not whether the house is good or bad. Both of you know that going into more debt is not going to help you be more financially responsible. The question is whether or not your marriage will be one in which you both trust each another. That is hard to accomplish when one of you is suggesting financial irresponsibility and the other goes along with it. Can you buy this house and be responsible and trustworthy?

Husband: No. In fact, to be irresponsible would be the reason to buy the house.

Therapist: Then this is the important question. Can you buy this house knowing what you know, and trust each other?

Husband: I see what you mean.

The therapy needs to confront how the couple currently uses money in order to find concrete ways in which that the partners can demonstrate responsibility with regard to financial matters. This often entails relating how they have oriented their behavior around the fear produced by money. Also, working through the following exercise can assist the couple in identifying their differences in orientations regarding the use of money and develop a balanced perspective for the relational "us" in using money in the future.

✒ *Couple Exercise Ten*

Using Money

Couples have four basic orientations regarding how to use money.

Money as Status
Money is used to symbolize power and success to society. The more money or material goods accumulated, the more the perception exists that one is powerful or successful.

Money as Security
Money is used as a means of protection. Potential fears or problems are dealt with by using financial resources as a barrier to the risks of everyday life.

Money as Enjoyment
Money is used to achieve satisfaction. Money is seen as a resource to spend on activities or goods that provide a sense of satisfaction and happiness for oneself or others.

Money as Control
Money is used as a means of maintaining independence. Preventing the individual or couple from becoming dependent on family or friends is a primary motivation.

All three orientations have positive aspects. We all want to have enough money to feel somewhat successful, to feel secure, to enjoy life a bit, and to feel as though we can manage our lives. Balance in motivation is the key. Knowing these orientations can help you individually and as a couple identify balanced ways to use money instead of fighting each other or developing bad financial patterns.

1. What is your individual orientation? How do you differ from your partner?
2. Are you currently responsible and trustworthy as a couple in the ways in which you handle finances? If not, what are some orientations that are out of balance?
3. How might you, as a couple, become more balanced?

Coping Skills

If the spouses are either overindulgers or underindulgers, the marriage is likely to encounter financial stress. If they differ on how each wants to use money, or if the partners are unbalanced as to its use, then financial problems are the result. But sometimes trustworthiness in the relational "us" will deteriorate further because of the coping strategy chosen to deal with the financial problems. Guadagno (1983) discusses four basic strategies that couples utilize in coping with their financial difficulties.

Increasing Family Income

This strategy is by far the most common choice of people who are stressed financially, overindulgent, or spending too much on status and enjoyment. Because a promotion or salary increase might be hard to achieve, most additional income is earned by taking a second job, working overtime, or having another family member find employment. All of these choices add further emotional stress to an insecure couple experiencing financial difficulty. Particularly with overindulgers, the response to this emotional stress is a tendency to spend even more money. Second, spouses spend less time together, although such time is essential if they are to come to an agreement on how to deal with the fear and use of money. Third, the stress of additional work in the family often produces resentment between the partners. This resentment deteriorates trust further and makes giving more unlikely.

There is, of course, nothing intrinsically wrong with taking a second job, in putting in overtime, or with both going to work. However, as even a short-term solution to financial problems created by the couple's instability, it often causes additional stress. In such situations, the therapist must encourage the spouses to care for each other emotionally and root out resentments so that they do not damage the couple's giving.

Decreasing Family Expenditures

Although this is a difficult strategy to master for couples dealing with money issues resulting from overindulging and imbalance, it is a much more responsible alternative. First, it helps the couple to face the reality of how to live without using money to promote their emotional happiness. Most would agree that money itself cannot make people happy, and living with the reality of not spending to comfort unhappiness trains the couple to give up the mythology that it can. Second, decreasing expenditures requires the couple to become more responsible in planning. This helps the spouses to take steps toward assessing their financial condition and finding out where each partner spends money. Finally, it creates a good habit for the couple. Spending patterns have usually developed over years, and sticking to a budget that decreases expenditures forces the development of new habits.

Spouses who decide to decrease family expenditures probably will need the therapist's assistance in setting up a financial plan that will (1) address the long-term problem of debt and (2) help them understand the fundamentals of record keeping and budgeting. The details of the budget will vary from couple to couple, and thus it is a good idea to seek the advice of a financial expert. In addition, the therapist must be a consistent source of encouragement. The budgeting activity and decreasing expenses develop baseline behaviors that result in both trust and stability in the marriage, but are difficult to maintain.

Extending the Resources on Hand

This strategy involves increasing the utility of our resources by using things until they are worn out and no longer can be repaired. This coping strategy is excellent for overindulgers who are used to replacing items at the first sign of trouble because this gives them an excuse to spend. It is also great for people who tend to spend money on material goods as evidence of an elevated status (a bigger house or more expensive car). But the therapist must also be aware that this strategy is sometimes used by underindulgers as an abusive mechanism to satisfy their need for security and control. Such was the case with a woman who was driving an 18-year-old automobile that was an apt candidate for the junkyard.

> "I no longer can depend on my car. It literally breaks down every other time I use it. My mechanic says that it is done for, and I know it is. He *(The husband)* drives a new car because he needs it in his business, and he keeps telling me that we can't afford another new one and I just have to repair the one I have. It is beyond repair. All he cares about is himself and he doesn't care if I get stranded. And if I talk about it too much, he explodes."

The therapist must always be aware of balance in terms of financial issues. Although most financial problems that are brought to therapy are a result of overspending and overindulgence, underspending and underindulgence can be just as damaging to trust and create just as much insecurity between partners. In such cases, the therapist must work to move the underindulging partner toward responsible and reliable spending that takes into account the reasonable good of the family.

Sharing

A fourth strategy that is available to couples in financial difficulty is sharing, or reciprocally borrowing goods and services from friends or extended family instead of making new purchases. Again, although this strategy is appropriate for some overspenders, it is a favored plan for facilitating underindulgers. The therapist must take care, however, to ensure that the proper boundaries around the sharing are intact and that the underindulger also engages in sharing. For instance, the underindulger must not put his or her spouse in an uncomfortable position of having to ask for something, and the balance between borrowing and giving among families must be fair. If I borrow your mower, I had better have an edger and a chain saw available when you need them.

Conclusions

Money issues can undermine the trust of a couple substantially and create enough stress to threaten the security of the relationship. In order to deal with these problems, the therapist first must ascertain whether the partners are overindulgent or underindulgent in dealing with their basic concerns and fears over money, and then move them to a more balanced perspective. Second, the therapist must help the couple come to a responsible and reliable agreement on how the relational "us" will use money. Although there are different emphases, it is reasonable to expect the couple to use money in a balanced way to meet security, status, enjoyment, and control needs. Finally, the therapist must help partners who have money problems to work through the coping strategies that have been chosen to ensure that they are effective and fair.

chapter nine

Raising Kids:
Parenting Issues in Marriage

Parenting is not for everyone, and it is not necessary to have children to ensure a happy marriage. Some 9% to 10% of couples choose not to have children, and those who do want offspring often delay child-bearing until the fourth decade of life (U.S. Bureau of the Census, 1994). Moreover, for those who do decide to have children, parenting issues can become a major concern for the marriage. For one thing, at each stage of their development, children have new demands. We do not have the option of ignoring babies or preschoolers or telling them to take care of themselves. It is up to us as parents to fulfill the needs of small children *as they develop those needs*. And as children grow, they have developmental problems to which parents must be sensitive in providing for their needs and in teaching them about life. Second, having children brings new relationships into the marriage. This not only is a complication because of the actual number of people now in the family, but it also gives spouses the opportunity to develop coalitions and bonds with the children that are closer than those with the other spouse. Third, children bring more strain on the family's economic, emotional, physical, and time resources. This is an expensive burden for parents to shoulder, in addition to their responsibilities for the marriage relationship, as well as such issues as individual growth, careers, and extended family.

So why would anyone who is aware of the many challenges involved opt to have children? No doubt some spouses became parents simply because they forgot to use or misused, their birth-control method. Others became parents for the wrong reason: perhaps one or both of the spouses felt lonely and wanted a friend. But there are also good reasons to have children. Some spouses want to bear children as a testimony to their faith in humanity—to give their best to make the world a better place and keep their legacies alive. Some wish to give of themselves in a selfless way for the good of another human being. Others want the opportunity to do better for their children than was done for them. There are many excellent reasons, but most relate to the spouses' giving of themselves for the good of the children, which, in turn, requires growth by the partners. One of the basic philosophies I have about all relationships is that they require us to grow up a little and learn more about ourselves. This is certainly true of marriage, and is also true of parenting. Parenting is not just about helping children grow up, it is also about growing up ourselves.

Parenting, perhaps more that any other "work" in marriage, reveals the quality of the "us" relationship. Biological children are by nature "between." They are literally and genetically new human beings created out of the "us" relationship of a man and a woman. Even nonbiological children carry this belonging to the relationship of the parents. The way that the parents cooperate in the care, nurture, discipline, and directing of a child is metaphorical for the resources that they have available to them in caring for the marital relationship. Although this may be different in a blended family, the principle of responsibly and reliably executing the job of parenting is representative of the partners' abilities to take responsibility for the "us" relationship.

But not everyone is successful in responsibly and reliably executing the job of spouse or parent. Irresponsible parenting can erode the marital relationship and an irresponsible marriage can take its toll on the parenting relationship. In either case, however, irresponsibility and unreliability create insecurity in the family relationships. For spouses to feel secure, they must believe that they can fulfill their obligations to the most important relational products of their marriage—their children. If they cannot get parenting right, the resulting insecurity destroys part of their marital "us-ness" and creates risk in the marriage. In therapy, there are three primary issues that contribute to the insecurity of the parenting relationship and thereby create problems in the marriage: problems with parenting styles, problems with the child's needs, and problems with individual and marital needs.

Therapy with Parenting Issues

Problems with Parenting Styles

Many problems in parenting stem from the spouses' differing styles of dealing with children. Parents love their children and want to do the best for them, but what they consider best may well come from how they themselves were parented. This logic takes two general forms. First, some parents choose their style out of *complacency*, meaning that they parent as they were parented because they believe that they themselves turned out okay. Second, some parents choose their style out of *reaction*, meaning that they parent in a way opposite to that of how they were parented because they believe that their own parents' style was damaging to them. In both cases, however, parents choose a style on the basis of their own experience, and not because the partner agrees or it is best for the child.

Baumrind (1991) has pioneered detailing the different styles of parenting. The four styles identified as a result of her work are authoritative, authoritarian, permissive, and rejecting. In addition, I believe it is helpful to delineate two other styles—an overinvolved style and a balanced style or involved style of parenting.

Authoritative Style

This style of parenting spells out roles and expectations very clearly to the children, but also allows them to dialogue and to provide input regarding rules and behaviors. Authoritative parents use reason and power to enforce their standards, but pay attention to a child's perspectives and concerns. Authoritative styles have been correlated with energetic, self-reliant, and achievement-oriented behavior in children.

Authoritarian Style

Authoritarian styles of parenting are rigid in the way that roles, rules, and expectations are set, and obedience is demanded of the children. Very little input or dialogue concerning the expectations are accepted by the parents. Authoritarian styles have been correlated with children who display conflicted, moody, unfriendly, and unhappy behavior.

Permissive Style

In permissive parenting, the child is allowed to set roles, rules, and expectations based on the basis of his or her preferences. The parent seldom voices clear expectations of the child and almost never uses power to prompt the child to adhere to a particular standard. Permissive styles have been correlated with impulsive, aggressive, rebellious, and underachieving behavior in children.

Rejecting Style

A parent with a rejecting style does not pay attention to the child's needs and does not set up clear roles or have particular expectations of the child, because the parent is too involved in meeting his or her own needs and wants. The parent basically rejects the role of parenting and takes little or no responsibility for being a parent. The child's presence has put the parent in the position of rejecting the responsibility, and so the child often feels unwanted. This often results in the child's having psychological problems, as well as being an underachiever.

Overinvolved Style

This type of parent is overly involved with a child. The child is never allowed to meet his or her own needs, and is never in a position to make decisions with regard to his or her own preferences. The overinvolved style of parenting produces children who are dependent, anxious, and underachieving.

Involved Style

This style of parenting is balanced in that it meets the needs of the child and, at the same time, takes responsibility for self-care and personal growth. The parent with an involved style is attentive to the child and helps the child to get his or her needs met, but is not necessarily the one who meets those needs. Because the child recognizes the balance, he or she displays respectful and resourceful behavior in relation to himself or herself and others.

In therapy, I find it helpful to conceptualize the first three styles by the idea of *rules, expectations, and enforcement.* In other words, how the parent will go about setting the rules and expectations for the child and how that parent will expect the child to obey is dominated by his or her authoritative, authoritarian, or permissive behavior. Authoritarian parents are rigid and demand complete obedience whereas permissive parents are chaotic and demand little. The balanced style is authoritative, and it consistently yields the best correlates in terms of child adjustment and behavior (Rueter & Conger, 1995). This balanced style is illustrated in Figure 9.1.

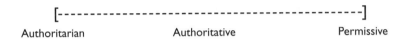

| Authoritarian | Authoritative | Permissive |

Figure 9.1 Balanced Style in Rules, Expectations, and Enforcement

I also find it helpful to conceptualize the latter three styles by the idea of *meeting needs and responsibilities.* If the parent is overly involved with meeting the needs of the child, the child never learns self-care and self-reliance. On the other hand, if the parent is only concerned about himself or herself, the child will feel unloved and unwanted because of the denial of care and nurture. The balanced involved style holds the potential for the parent to balance personal needs with parental responsibility, while teaching the child hopeful and self-reliant care. This balance is illustrated in Figure 9.2.

| Rejecting | Involved | Overinvolved |

Figure 9.2 Balanced Style in Meeting Needs and Responsibilities

When parents have different or imbalanced styles, they create difficulties in the way that they influence their children, but they also become critical of each other. Remember, each probably believes that his or her style of parenting is correct. When there are problems with the children, they see each other as irresponsible or unreliable in fulfilling expectations, and will often blame each other. I find that when spouses are informed about the various styles of parenting and which yields the best correlates of child behavior, they usually choose to parent in a healthier style. Such a style makes good heuristic sense, and the couple almost always feels the rightness of the balanced style. This opens them up to the idea of parent education and to the techniques and behaviors that will make them better parents. I usually use the following exercise to assist couples with this process.

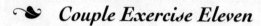 *Couple Exercise Eleven*

Parenting Styles

We are all affected by our past and we sometimes develop a parenting style that reflects our beliefs of what our children need. Read through the following styles.

Authoritative Style

This style of parenting spells out very clear roles and expectations to the children, but allows the child to dialogue and to have input concerning rules and behaviors. Authoritative parents use reason and power to enforce their standards, but pay attention to the child's perspectives and concerns. Authoritative styles have been correlated with energetic, self-reliant, and achievement-oriented behavior in children.

Authoritarian Style

Authoritarian styles of parenting are rigid in the way that roles, rules, and expectations are set and obedience is demanded. Very little input or dialogue concerning the expectations are accepted by the parent. Authoritarian styles have been correlated with children who display conflicted, moody, unfriendly, and unhappy behavior.

Permissive Style

The permissive style of parenting allows the child to set roles, rules, and expectations on the basis of the child's own preference. Parents with this style seldom have clear expectations of the child, and almost never use power to prompt the child to adhere to a particular standard. Permissive styles have been correlated with impulsive, aggressive, rebellious, and underachieving behavior in children.

Rejecting Style

A rejecting parent does not pay attention to the child's needs and does not have clear roles or expectations of the child because the parent is too involved in meeting his or her own needs and wants. In this style, the parent basically rejects the role of parenting and takes little or no responsibility in being a parent. The child's presence has put the parent in the position of rejecting the responsibility, so the child often feels unwanted. This often results in the child's having serious psychological problems, as well as being an underachiever.

Overinvolved Style

This type of parent is overly involved with the child. The child is basically never left to meet his or her own needs and is never in a position to make decisions with regard to his or her own preferences. The overinvolved style produces children that are dependent, anxious, and underachieving.

Involved Style

This style of parenting is balanced in that it meets the needs of the child and, at the same time, takes responsibility for self-care and personal growth. The involved parent is attentive to the child and helps the child get his or her needs met, but is not necessarily the one who meets those needs. Because the child recognizes the balance, he or she displays respectful and resourceful behavior in relation to himself or herself and others.

It is helpful to look at the first three styles of how you parent with regard to setting rules, expressing expectations, and enforcing consequences on your child's behavior. The latter three styles are more reflective of your style of balancing your own needs with the needs of your child and how you fulfill your parental responsibility. In both of the following illustrations, it is important to remember that a balanced style is the best.

Style in Setting Rules, Expressing Expectations, and Enforcing Consequences

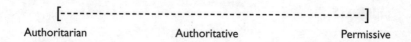

| Authoritarian | Authoritative | Permissive |

1. Where along the continuum do you and your spouse land? What would be a healthier style for both of you to adopt?

Style in Balancing Parental and Child Needs and Responsibilities

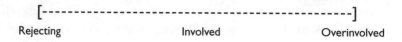

| Rejecting | Involved | Overinvolved |

1. Where along the continuum do you and your spouse land? What would be a healthier style for both of you to adopt?
2. In both sets of styles, how do you propose to move, or get help to move, to a more balanced style?

Problems with the Child's Needs

Many of the difficulties that parents have in meeting their responsibilities and obligations regarding their children are related to the child's needs. Every child is a unique individual, and each has a different personality and will respond to parenting differently. However, many parents do not have even a basic understanding of what their children need in terms of family life. I divide childhood into three developmental elements to help parents get a handle on the idea of how children mature and what they require from parenting. These elements involve the goals of fostering the child's healthy self-esteem, giving the child an understanding of cooperation and boundaries, and helping the child grow into a responsible and self-reliant adult. When I ask parents what they want for their children, most will give answers that resemble these three goals in one form or another. I try to move the parents to see that the goal of their childrearing will be to meet the child's needs at each stage in order to help the child develop.

Healthy Self-Esteem

From age 0 to 5 years, the child experiences the most dramatic growth of his or her life. Infants go from being totally dependent and vulnerable to being preschoolers with aggressive drives toward identity and expression. Whether personality and behavior are a result of nature or nurture, the child looks to the family environment and the family to confirm his or her existence and worth. The child is seeking to answer the question, "Who am I?"

The child will by and large answer that question according to how the child is loved by the parents. If they love the child unconditionally and are willing to sacrifice themselves for his or her good, the child will feel special and worthy. If the parents love the child in such a way that his or her existence is celebrated, then the child will feel precious. If we want to raise children who will feel good about themselves, then we must love them unconditionally, bond and attach to them, and cherish them.

Cooperation and Boundaries

From age 6 to age 10, the child is developing physically and learning about his or her skills and talents, and is also developing socially and learning how to govern his or her behavior. The child learns about how that behavior affects others, experiences progress or obstacles in trying to attain goals, and consolidates moral and gender identities. Basically, the child is learning how to act in society and is asking, "How should I act toward others?"

Parents can help a child answer this question by setting good boundaries and enforcing appropriate consequences for behaviors. When children act in trustworthy and responsible ways with regard to boundaries, they learn to cooperate, which results in personal benefits and rewards. However, if boundaries are too rigid, or are nonexistent, the child is confused and neither matures nor learns to cooperate. A parent who disciplines and encourages the child by setting appropriate limits helps the child learn how to be trustworthy.

Responsible and Self-Reliant

Parenting, if done properly, is a job that should demand less and less involvement as the child grows closer to adulthood. From the age of 11 to 18 years, children must learn to develop their adult identities and to become responsible for themselves. Adolescence is a time where the child will try out different roles in search of an adult identity that integrates some of what the parents possess, but is distinctly that of the child. The problem is, of course, that the adolescent oscillates between taking an independent adultlike stance and being very immature.

During this stage of development, the parental role is to hand over greater control to the child so that the child can experience the responsibility and self-reliance of an adult. This hand-off of responsibility starts slowly at the beginning of adolescence with the setting of good boundaries, rules, and structures, but more and more is left to the adolescent to develop as he or she approaches maturity. In other words, good parenting at this stage is learning how to let go so the child can become an adult.

Under this paradigm, the three developmentally appropriate parenting behaviors are to love the child unconditionally, to set good boundaries and enforce consequences, and to let go and allow the child to become an adult. Of course, a good parent practices all three of these throughout the child's childhood. For instance, with my children, who are ages 10 and 8, I now concentrate on setting good boundaries and consequences, but certainly I am still striving to love them unconditionally. Also, I increasingly allow them to play by themselves or to take bike rides alone. I utilize all three parenting skills, but just rely on one or the other more heavily, depending on the child's particular stage of development.

In therapy, many parents create insecurity and produce conflicts with their children because their parenting emphasis is developmentally inappropriate. Many times, these problems then result in insecurity in the marital relationship because the parents blame each other or are at odds with each other concerning what they should do. Such was the case with a woman and man who had been married for 26 years and had a 14-year-old daughter who was defiant and oppositional in many ways, and was becoming increasingly disobedient.

> Wife: You are always on her *(the daughter)* about everything. She is just mad at you because you never were there to cuddle and hold her. You have always been hard and demanding, always pointing out what she did wrong. You never point out what is right.

Husband: And I always feel as though you take her side in everything. I set a rule and she breaks it. You never try to hold her responsible for any of her behavior. You never have. Ever since the kids were little, you would let them run all over you.

Wife: I felt like I had to do that because you were so hard.

Husband: I felt like I had to be harder because you would never set limits or discipline them.

In this case, the husband and wife were letting each other's parenting and misinformation distract them from their daughter's needs. The mother loved the daughter dearly, but was hesitant to set the appropriate boundaries and enforce the consequences necessary if the daughter were to learn responsible and cooperative behavior. On the other hand, the father failed to express his love to his daughter when she was a preschooler, and he now wanted to deal with her adolescent behavior by becoming more rigid and making more rules. The parents were simply out of sync with what the daughter needed to become an adult.

I find that it is helpful to educate couples with regard to these three simple stages of development and to assist them in making the appropriate changes to facilitate meeting a child's needs. As they identify the needs and appropriate behavior, then they can focus on working together, no matter how the child behaves. This working together in a trustworthy way contributes to the couple's security in their own relationship.

❧ *Couple Exercise Twelve*

Dealing with Parenting Issues

Parenting is a lifelong activity. Many conflicts in marriages are caused by the parents' different ways of dealing with the children. Children do best and feel most secure, however, when parents agree on issues and present a bonded and united parenting front. One of the best guides to parenting children is to (1) help develop healthy self esteem, (2) construct cooperative boundary behavior, and (3) develop responsible and self-reliant entrance into adulthood.

Healthy Self-Esteem (Ages 0 to 5)
All that children know about themselves comes from the way in which they are loved. You must love a child unconditionally to teach him or her that he or she is unique, precious, deserving, and special.

Cooperation and Boundaries (Ages 6 to 10)
Children learn responsibility from dealing with the consequences of right and wrong actions. You must provide your child with limits and boundaries that result in consequences for misbehavior if your child is to become responsible in society.

Responsibility and Self-Reliance (Ages 11 to —)
There comes a time when children must start making their own choices and live as adults. You must sever ties with your children to facilitate their entrance into an adult world. This means you must not "bail them out" of their difficulties or try to make their decisions for them.

1. How are you and your spouse different in your beliefs about parenting?
2. Are there areas where you both could become more responsible and more reliable parents? List some of those ways.
3. Try to use the following questions to help formulate a plan of parenting upon which both can agree.

   • How do you feel you need to show your child love?
   • What are some appropriate limits and consequences your child needs?
   • How do you need to "back off" and allow your child to grow?

Problems with Individual and Marital Needs

Parenting is a taxing job. It can also take up all of one's time. As discussed earlier, many spouses have a style of parenting that is either rejecting of the child's needs or is too overinvolved. A parent with a balanced, or involved, style of parenting pays attention to the needs and responsibilities of the adult, as well as those of the child.

Most partners who are parents are subject to an enormity of marital demands. Miller and Myers-Walls (1983) point out several adult and couple issues that arise around the task of parenting. First, individual partners face demands on their time and energy resources because of the need to produce income, just when the time is crucial for advancing their careers, discharging community or civic responsibilities, and engaging in hobbies or personal growth. At the same time, the demands of marriage present further time and stress issues. The couple must learn how to adjust the marital dyad to accommodate children and must share their love with the children. The partners must struggle with finding time to develop their marriage and deal with the stress that less time produces in the form of poorer communication, ebbs in marital satisfaction, and errors in decision making. These individual and couple demands, when combined with the stress of parenting, can produce problems in the marital "us-ness."

In therapy, I often see spouses who have developed insecurity in the marital relationship because they were out of balance with regard to the individual/marital needs and the needs of their children. Only in a few instances have I seen a rejecting style on the parts of both parents. A more common style is for both parents to be overly involved in meeting the needs of the child, while neglecting their responsibilities to themselves and the marriage. In these cases, one or both of the partners eventually tire of the demands of parenting or find that parenting cannot give them the emotional nurture and care they want from a spouse. Dissatisfaction with the relationship grows and becomes more complex as the child receives less and less care from the parents. A child of these types of parents is often triangulated into the parental relationship as he or she becomes the only common denominator of spousal interest. As the child then tries to grow and extricate himself or herself to establish adulthood, the marital bond becomes more insecure and untrustworthy.

But by far the most common type of involvement that produces problems is for one spouse to be rejecting while the other is overly involved. In such situations, the rejecting spouse becomes inattentive to his or her parental responsibilities and concentrates on work, a career, hobbies, or friends outside the family. On the other hand, the overinvolved spouse dedicates himself or herself to being attentive to every need or activity of the child, while paying little attention to his or her own growth and development. In these cases, the marital security deteriorates dramatically because the obligations and responsibilities of the marriage have not been fulfilled. This was the situation with a couple that had been married for 20 years and whose children were in their early adolescence.

Husband: I am functionally a stranger in my own home. You ignore me and the kids treat me like the provider.

Wife: It is because they don't know you. You work all the time, and when you come home, you barely say a word. They want to know you, but they don't know how.

Husband: All I am is a money bag. I work all the time to keep this family in the green. *(Pause)* There isn't much appreciation.

Wife: I do appreciate what you do, but we need your time.

Therapy must move the couple to meet their obligations to each other and the relational "us" in a responsible and reliable way. In this case, the therapist works to confront the spouses with the need to become more balanced in the way they meet needs and to rebuild trustworthiness between them.

Therapist: *(To the wife)* You said, "We need your time." What do you mean by we?

Wife: I meant me and the children.

Therapist: *(To the husband)* I know that the children do need you. You have things that only fathers can give their children. You may be used to just giving money, but you also must learn to give them part of yourself. *(To the wife)* But I want to ask you, do you need your husband's time apart from your children?

Wife: *(Pause)* I haven't thought about that in a long time. I am so use to thinking about the children and me together.

Therapist: I am sure that's true. I am sure that you are a very attentive mother to your children. But you also have a responsibility as a wife, apart from the mothering role. It seems that the marriage has been put on hold while you fulfill your parental role.

Wife: That may be true.

Husband: I know that's true.

Therapist: *(To the husband)* But I think that you have probably also put your marriage on hold.

Husband: How so?

Therapist: You have been so busy giving yourself to work and career that it is hard to see how you need your marriage. You seem to spend very little time on it.

Husband: That's probably true, but it's not because I don't want it. I feel hopeless that I can get her back to being involved with me.

Therapist: What you both need is to think about getting back into balance. You *(the husband)* must be more attentive to your parenting role. You *(the wife)* must be less focused on your parenting role. More responsible, less responsible. But both of you must be responsible for starting to take care of each other and developing your marital relationship. Both of you seem to be shirking your responsibility to give your partner what he or she needs. Neither of you should use work or kids as an excuse anymore.

Conclusions

Parenting poses a substantial task for marital partners and can produce enormous distrust between them. In order to assist a couple in dealing with security issues surrounding parenting, the therapist can help them to identify differing or out-of-balance parenting styles. Achieving this balance not only makes them better parents, but it creates more family stability. Second, the therapist can help the couple by educating them concerning the developmental needs of the child. This need not be detailed, but the parents require enough information so they can help their children to have healthy self-esteems, to respect and respond to boundaries, and to become more self-reliant as they approach adulthood. Finally, helping the partners to balance the demands of parenting and the responsibilities of the marital relationship can assist them in being more reliable to their "us."

chapter ten

Insulting Trust: Surviving Sexual Infidelity

L isten to the pain:

> When my husband had the affair, it was like someone was coming in
> to cut off my limbs. No, it was like being awake while your arms
> were being cut off. There is mess everywhere and the pain is unbear-
> able. You want to clean up the mess, but your arms are gone. You
> scream and fight, but part of you is being cut away. There is nothing
> to do but wait until the carnage is over. Then when it is over, you are
> permanently marred. You are forever changed in a way that you did-
> n't choose or want to be. It hurts, it's hard, and it's forever. It's like
> having your life napalmed.

When we talk about infidelity, we need to remember that it is a terrible thing that causes a great damage to people's lives. The pain of this
woman's story is not unique; most people whose spouses are sexually
unfaithful feel just as much pain. It's insecurity that results from sexual
infidelity that has such a devastating effect on a marriage. Infidelity is one
of the major reasons why marriages fail (Albrecht, 1979). But failed marriages are only part of the story of infidelity. Extramarital sex strikes at
the very heart of the "us" relationship and destroys it. If "us" survives on
love and trust between partners, infidelity calls love into question and
devastates trust. It is not just a matter of the spouses staying together.

Their lives are disrupted and sometimes destroyed by the emotional, financial, social, and relational turmoil. Affairs can destroy relationships, whether the couple eventually divorces or stays together. No matter how we frame affairs, they are abusive and destructive to the human beings involved and to the "us" relationship.

When spouses come to therapy because one of them has had an affair, we need to acknowledge that the insecurity stemming from the destruction of trust is very serious. At the same time, we as therapists need to be confident that many couples do survive sexual infidelity. But, as therapists, we also must be clear on the problem and abuse—and the road to recovery—that sexual infidelity represents in marriage.

The Problem

It is extraordinarily difficult to ascertain the true frequency of marital infidelity. Kinsey and his associates estimated that 50% of husbands and 26% of wives engage in at least one extramarital affair (Kinsey, Pomeroy, Martin, & Gebhard, 1953). Glass and Wright (1992) put the estimates at 44% for men and 25% for women. But the variance in percentages is wider, ranging from 72% of men and 70% of women (Hite, 1989) to 21% of men and 12% of women (Smith, 1993). The differences in these estimates are attributable in part to problems in sampling and the setting in which the information was gathered. So it is probably realistic to assume that the rate of infidelity is somewhere between 30% and 55% for men and between 25% and 40% for women. When we talk about marital infidelity, we cannot assume that all the male and female infidels are married to one another. This means that the combined percentages for men and women probably indicates that at least 50% of marriages are marked by at least one infidelity during their course.

Although it is true that all infidelity strikes at the heart of the "us" relationship, some infidelities are more likely to destroy a marriage. Humphrey (1987) has developed a useful categorization of extramarital sex that takes into account time, the amount of emotional involvement, the presence of sexual intercourse, the degree of secrecy involved, whether a single or multiple infidelities, and whether heterosexual or homosexual infidelity. It makes good sense that the "one-night stand" will affect the relationship differently than will an infidel who has had many secret affairs or one where there has been a single affair involving a strong emotional attachment. However, the impact of the infidelity has the same sense of betrayal, even though the degree may be different.

The Abuse

One of my major concerns about infidelity in marriage is the seeming ambivalence that we as mental health profession have toward affairs. We think that in order to be nonjudgmental and accepting of people as people, we must accept whatever behavior they exhibit in relationships. I personally think that it is unrealistic and misinformed to view relational abuse in the form of affairs in this way, even though my position is not very politically correct. We would not tolerate spouses' perpetrating physical violence on each other, such as choking, twisting arms, or punching each other in the face, because we know that physical violence damages both individuals and relationships. Why then do we refuse to take a strong position against extramarital affairs? We can document just as much emotional pain and as much devastation for families from affairs as from violence.

Rarely do therapists realize the pain that people feel when a spouse breaks the vow of fidelity and has sex with someone else. As a profession, we have come very close to what I believe is excusing affairs by our silence and failure to confront their damage. Our excuses usually come in two forms. First, we tend to look at affairs as "creative communication" to the marriage that something is wrong. This logic goes back to the systemic belief that all actions are communication in the family. Although it is true that many affairs are the result of marital problems, they, by their nature, violate trust. There is always a better way to communicate problems within the relationship. To insinuate that both relational partners are responsible for an affair fails to recognize the gravity of that violation. Both spouses are responsible for a bad marriage, but that does not mean that both are responsible for infidelity. To say that affairs are just another way for spouses to communicate their unhappiness is to say that a person who robs a bank is just trying to communicate that he or she is poor and in need of a loan.

The other common excuse that I find among therapists is that affairs are simply unavoidable realities of marriage. The logic of this excuse goes something like this. Love, especially romantic love, tends to disappear from marriage and, as the years go by, marital satisfaction wanes. But love, especially romantic love, is essential to individual happiness. Although the partners may accept the obligations and responsibilities of their marriages, the desire, love, and happiness may cause them to pursue an extramarital affair to satisfy their longings. There is little that we, as professionals, can do but be supportive of people's choices and help them deal with the reality of the damaging fallout.

Is monogamy then an illusion? If we mean by that that monogamy is the standard of marriage, yes, monogamy is an illusion. Most marriages are probably not monogamous. There is a better question, however. Is monogamy an essential part of the marital bond? The answer here must be a resounding Yes. An overwhelming number of people disapprove of extramarital sex and expect their marriages to be monogamous. Victims of affairs will often undergo recurrent trauma that brings back their distress over the event, its discovery, or the secrecy involved. Sleep disturbances, with distressing dreams, often recur. Victims may obsessively ruminate about the affair, which with may result in irritability, anger, difficulty concentrating, hypervigilance, or depression (Lusterman, 1995). We cannot say that monogamy guarantees a good marital relationship, but we can say that infidelity guarantees marital insecurity.

I think that much of our problem in this area stems from our societal confusion about sex, and especially extramarital sex. The media glamorize sex and affairs, painting an unrealistic picture of how extramarital relationships can be exciting and can satisfy our unfulfilled desires. Combine this with our bias over the last 50 years that an individual's happiness and satisfaction of his or her own passions are justified and necessary for his or her self-actualization, and we have developed a belief system under which, if people feel it is necessary to sacrifice their families for what they want, then they are doing what they must do by having an affair.

One of the reasons I was so attracted to family therapy in the first place was the sense of balance so eloquently expressed in our theories. The balance of individuality or autonomy and the drive for togetherness is essential to health. If marriage is to do well in the next millennium, it will be because we forge a new commitment to monogamy that is committed to individual and relational needs in balance—not one at the expense of the other.

Affairs cause marital destruction and, as professionals, we must take a stand against this type of relational abuse. However, I am not suggesting that we condemn everyone who has an affair. I am suggesting that, as a profession, we have an obligation to strive not only for individual health, but also for relational health. We can understand individuals' desires for gratification and fulfillment. We can recognize that some relationships will not work. We can even help people to work through infidelity. But first, we must be clear that infidelity is destructive to everybody concerned.

Security After Sexual Infidelity

How do we go about dealing with infidelity effectively in therapy and restoring security to the marriage. In my opinion, there are three primary issues with which a couple must deal after an affair. These center around love, trust, and power, as shown in Figure 10.1. However, it is not a simple process. When a marriage suffers an infidelity, the relationship is flooded by a host of issues. These must be sorted out, and then the couple must balance the triad—love, trust, and power—in order to recover from the effects of the infidelity.

Love

Trust   Power

Figure 10.1 Balanced Ingredients of Recovery from Infidelity

Love

When infidelity occurs, the question of love is unavoidable. Listen to a 38-year-old man as he cries out in anguish after learning that his wife of 12 years had had an affair.

> How could she do this to me? I loved her with all my heart. I was com-
> mitted to her with all my heart. What was it about me that wasn't
> enough for her? How could she love someone else?

We depend on the way people love us to tell us who we are—to tell us
that we are special, unique, and, most important, worthy of love. We
should get most of this in our family-of-origin, but after that, most of us
look to a spouse to provide us with the love and companionship we need.
When someone we love is unfaithful, we can only ask ourselves, "What
is wrong with me? Can I ever love and give to my spouse again? Can I
ever believe that my spouse loves me?"

But the questions are not limited to the victim of the infidelity. The
infidels themselves have tough questions about love that must be
answered. Some infidelity refers to a one-night stand where there is no
emotional connection between the lovers, but takes place in a setting of
romantic love and emotional intimacy. The unfaithful spouse has to confront his or her feelings for the lover while dealing with how love and
connection will affect the other spouse. "Do I love my spouse enough to
go back? Can my spouse ever fulfill me? Can I make a life with my lover,
and how would I know that love is secure?"

For the victim of an infidelity, the questions of love must be the first to
be sorted out, a difficult task in view of the many different emotions
involved—among them, rage, hate, hurt, sadness, and depression. Here is
a young man trying to deal with these emotions.

> This is killing me. When I think of my wife with another man I want
> to throw up. I would like to find this guy and kick him through the
> wall the way I've been kicked. Then I think, this is my own fault. If
> I had been a better husband, she wouldn't have gone to this guy. I've
> been tempted myself, so I know what it's like. But still, I didn't do it.
> I can't believe that she did. I love her and I want her, and at the same
> time, I hate her.

As a therapist, you have to latch on to the roller coaster and stay with
the victims as they ride out the turbulence. But you also have to bring
them back to the question of their love for their spouses. I ask the victims
to focus on their love for their unfaithful spouse, and to be realistic about

the fact that they will have to move past the rage and anger if they choose to stay in the relationship. I ask them to think about the original reasons they loved their spouses and help them to collect the love that remains. This is an essential task of therapy, because they will have to depend on this love to mitigate their anger over the insult of the infidelity. In essence, I ask them to look past the infidelity and all the pain it has caused to what was or is good in the marriage.

Romantic love is intoxicating and recovery from affairs is difficult. After an affair, I try to make it clear that if spouses are going to be reconciled, the relationship with the lover must be ended completely. Otherwise, it leaves the lover with the hope that if things don't work out, the affair can be resumed. Here is an excerpt from a session where a man described his efforts to put an end to an eight-month affair.

Therapist: You cut off the relationship with this woman? *(Husband nods)* Tell me about how it went.

Husband: I told her that I just can't throw away 13 years of marriage without being sure that it won't work. I told her that I'm totally committed to seeing if we can get the problems worked out in the marriage and if I can love my wife. If it doesn't work, then I'll move on with my life.

Therapist: *(Pause)* If it doesn't work out.... *(Pause)* How long do you feel it will take you to see if you can love your wife?

Husband: About three or four months.

Therapist: *(Long pause)* What then?

Husband: *(Long pause)* I guess I would hope that if I'm not able to work it out with my wife, I could go back to her and she would take me back.

Therapist: You would pick up where you left off?

Husband: Yeah.

Therapist: Do you believe that she *(the other woman)* knows that you have left this door open?

Husband: We didn't talk about it, but I believe she will wait to see what happens to my marriage.

Therapist: This is difficult. I know that you have made an effort to end this relationship, but I wonder if what you are doing with this woman is just giving yourself some time to make a more graceful exit from your marriage and you really are not all that committed to making it work. If you were, I don't think you would leave the door open.

Husband: *(Long pause)* I think you are right.

It is an absolute essential for the infidel to cut off any relationship with the lover. This cutoff must include the overt action of telling the lover that even if the marriage ends in divorce, their relationship is over. This clean break sets the stage for directing the affection of the infidel, even if minimal, back toward the spouse. Spouses who are victims of affairs have enough problems believing that they are loved without having to face the competition of a lover.

Trust

Questions of love are difficult after infidelity, but trust is the primary target of damage. To engage in the free giving that an intimate bond demands, you must believe that your spouse will reciprocate. You cannot give in relationships if you get nothing in return. It is not that we don't love enough, but we have a built-in perception of justice. Trustworthiness is based on fairness or justice. If I give love, security, and nurture, and my spouse does nothing, my sense of justice will be insulted and I will feel angry. If my spouse gives love, nurture, and security to me, and I do nothing, then my sense of justice will be attacked and I will feel guilty. But angry or guilty, when giving is not balanced, I can no longer rely on my spouse and I start looking out for myself. I stop giving, and start threatening or manipulating. Trust evaporates and the "us-ness" of our relationship is in jeopardy.

Victims of affairs will ask, "How can I ever be sure of my spouse again? How can I be sure he or she won't do it again?" In working with couples to rebuild trust, it is important that both the partners be realistic. Trustworthiness is neither a promise nor a guarantee. Victims can never be sure that their spouses won't be unfaithful again, just as infidels can never be sure that their spouses will forgive them. Trustworthiness is a resource that accumulates over time to allow people to deal with each other based on realistic and valid assumptions and demonstrations of past reliability.

I look at the rebuilding of trustworthiness in two phases. In the first phase, the infidel must come clean about the affair, as well as any other past affairs and any other secrets that have been kept from the spouse. This always means painful revelations about the emotions surrounding the affair and the degree of the involvement. The amount of information that victims of infidelity need about the affair varies. Some want all the details and others feel more comfortable with just hearing the admission without the details. I let the victim decide how much or how little he or she wants to know. This usually makes for a difficult session, but the victim needs to see that the infidel clearly understands that the information to which he or she must admit caused damage and hurt. He or she needs to see that the unfaithful spouse regrets the actions, and intends to remain faithful in the future. Honesty forces the infidel to take these courageous steps of recognizing, regretting, and, for lack of a better word, repenting.

The honesty serves the function of getting the worst out into the open. The second phase of rebuilding trust then begins. I start this process by having the infidel agree to report his or her whereabouts when not at home. Many people resist doing this because they feel that once an affair has been revealed, life should get back to normal. However, the truth is that trust between the couple must be reconditioned. One way to do this is not to make the victim have to guess whether the unfaithful spouse is actually working late or if errands are really being run. Some victimized spouses also resist this type of reporting, believing that they should be able to trust the other spouse. Although I encourage the effort, I try to make the victim see trust building in a more realistic way, as a goal that reporting will assist in achieving. Building trustworthiness is like reestablishing a credit line after a bankruptcy. If I declared bankruptcy and then asked my local bank for a loan of, say, $20,000 to purchase a new car, I would be refused. But if I requested a $200 loan that I would pay back over four weeks, my banker would probably take the chance. If I then asked for a $400 loan that I would pay back in two months, once again I might be successful. If I faithfully paid back the loans on time while I increased the amount of money borrowed, at the end of a year or 18 months, I might be able to borrow $6,000 to buy a used car. I had proved my trustworthiness. Most of the time, we can use a simple contract in order to make this reporting easier. It would require cell phone contact several times during the day, or within 10 minutes if the person is not where he or she was supposed to be. It is best that the unfaithful spouse does not leave town alone for at least a year, and that the victimized spouse has the right to "drop in" on the other spouse at any time. Contact between the spouses should be maximized during this time.

In cases where the spouses have to be separated because of professional or other obligations, Fred DiBlasio of the University of Maryland suggests putting away $800 to $1,000 at the victim's disposal to be used, if necessary, to hire a private investigator to follow the spouse. This not only reassures the victim, but helps the infidel to resist temptation and thus win back the confidence of the other spouse.

These measures are intended to be short term, but might last anywhere from 6 to 18 months. As the spouse proves trustworthiness, the other spouse can invest more trust in the situation and risk more. When the anger or depression starts to subside, the couple can begin the work of changing the status of the relationship. When an affair is the result of an unsatisfactory relationship, the relationship must change. But even if the relationship was good before the affair, it must be recognized that it is different now and that love and trust must be restored. Marital therapy means identifying the couple's destructive patterns, moving the spouses to effective communication and problem solving, and securing a commitment to a new "us-ness."

To rebuild trust is to rebuild the heart of the relationship. But even in the best-case scenarios, it is a two-steps-forward, one-step-back process. When trustworthiness is proved, the pain will fade with time, but the infidelity will never be completely forgotten. It is impossible to forgive and forget, but it is possible to forgive and trust again.

Power

who is in control of the rel?

I used to concentrate only on discovering the reservoir of love with a couple and rebuilding trust, but I have found that it is also essential to address the issue of power with the spouses if they are going to be able to move past an infidelity. By power, I mean who is in control of the relationship. Remember, the triad of love, trust, and power must be in balance to heal marital infidelity. If power is not tempered by love and justice, which are the basis of trust, then people misuse their power. Does absolute power corrupt absolutely? I do not know, but I do know that power without love and trust usually results in exploitation, and then revenge.

There are several patterns of power that I see in relationships that have suffered infidelity. First, the infidel recognizes the damage that he or she has caused to the relationship, feels guilty, and wants to reconcile with the spouse. I believe that a little guilt is good when you do wrong. But this pattern puts the infidel in a one-down position where the victim gets to call the shots. The victim decides whether or not to forgive and whether the relationship will continue. I think this is a good situation for about a month because it puts the victimizer in the position of being willing to go the extra mile to rebuild love and trust with his or her spouse. But if the victim welds total power for too long, the infidel begins to wonder what's in it for him or her. "Does my wrong mean that I will have to spend my entire life always trying to make up for it? When is enough guilt enough? Do I have to live with a tyrant because of a past mistake?" Most people, even if they are truly sorry for having had an affair, will eventually give up because they feel that they aren't rebuilding a relationship, but only bearing a cross.

Another common pattern is when a partner who held the reins prior to having an affair tries to maintain that position after the infidelity. Quite frankly, I have never seen any good come out of these situations. In these relationships, the unfaithful spouse believes that he or she can do whatever he or she pleases, and that the spouse simply has to take it. Listen to this 32-year-old man's lame defense of his long history of infidelities to his wife.

> I know that affairs are wrong, but I can't help myself. Men are built differently than women. Men evolved to inseminate as many women as possible, it's genetic. It doesn't mean that I don't love you when I slip up. I'm really trying. I am still a good husband and you really do need me, not only financially, but also to help you keep your head on straight.

As a man, I find this statement offensive. But I also have heard similar absurd and offensive excuses from women. Listen to this explanation from a 44-year-old woman to her 46-year-old husband as she leaned over and stuck her finger into his face.

I don't want to hear any more about my affairs. I have only had three the whole time we've been married. I have had your children, I am raising them, and I have to put up with you. I do pretty good. You don't have any business trying to pry into my love life.

In these situations, where the infidel in the one-up position tries to hold on to that position, I seldom find any kind of reconciliation of the relationship. If the relationship does go on, then it is only because the victim of the infidelity rolls over and takes it. The relationship is totally void of trustworthiness and the "us-ness" is murdered off. It simply does not work.

So how should the power between the spouses be aligned? After a very short period during when the victim is in control, the power must be redistributed equally. This is perhaps the biggest change a couple suffering infidelity will undergo. No more does one or the other hold the upper hand, but they must share power, and this means communicating, deciding together how issues in the relationship will be handled, and developing respect for each other's current contributions. This means that although both partners in the relationship may make mistakes, both also have value.

Another issue concerning power is secrecy. One of the most effective ways to equalize power for spouses when one has been unfaithful is to teach them to be honest about their sexual thoughts. That is, if one of them finds himself or herself consistently being attracted to another person or entertaining sexual fantasies, that information should be shared with the other spouse. Once the information is out, the secret loses its power. Imagine how many affairs could be avoided if, for instance, a husband told his wife, "I am really attracted to a woman in my office and I find myself flirting. I'm telling you this so you will know and I won't be tempted." Honesty works and undoes the power of the secret sexual obsession.

Conclusions

Sexual infidelity is a severe blow to the relational "us" and destroys security because it destroys trust. However, relationships can be restored and security can be recaptured. To accomplish this task in therapy, three essential things must be accomplished. First, the issues concerning love must be settled among the victim, the infidel, and the lover. Second, trust in the marriage relationship must be rebuilt. This is difficult, but can be done through responsible, reliable, and sequential behavior. Trust is essentially rebuilt a little at a time over a long period (Hargrave, 1994). Finally, the holding of power by the two spouses eventually must be equalized. These three essentials must be dealt with and balanced to be effective in helping a couple to recover from an infidelity.

Section IV

Growing a Strong and Sincere "Us"

chapter eleven

Sincerity and Growth in the Marriage

One more mental image of the couple in the rowboat. The spouses have achieved a sense of stability, meaning that they do not hurt each other and can exist in the same space. They have learned how to row together in rhythm and to accomplish the work of marriage in terms of careers, maintenance, parenting, and the emotional nurturing required to ensure a sense of marital security. The marital "us-ness" is safe, responsible, and reliable. They are good partners in terms of feeling comfortable next to one another. They have learned how to accommodate to each other's style. This kind of safety and security in the relational "us" allows the spouses to look at each other and say, "Where would you like 'us' to go? What kind of dreams and hopes do you have? Guess what I have learned about myself during this journey of rowing with you." In short, they start exploring the "us-ness" in their relationship in an effort to grow, individually and relationally.

Sincerity, as used here, is much more than honesty or integrity, although it certainly includes those two ideas. *Sincerity is the ability to learn about oneself in the context of the marital relationship.* It is the notion that as a person gives himself or herself to the marital "us," he or she more and more sees the value of nurturing the relationship instead of just nurturing himself or herself. He or she begins to realize that being a marital partner actually reveals the strengths and weaknesses of his or her own personhood and behavior. As one gives of oneself to make a relationship stronger, one becomes a better and stronger person. Remember Keiffer's (1977) statement about intimacy? As a result of the bond of intimacy, we end up knowing ourselves better. This is what sincerity is about. When we start participating in a loving and trustworthy relationship not because of what we can get, but because of what we want to give, we do so because we have learned that by giving ourselves, we attain a stronger, more loving, and more trustworthy relationship, and we become stronger, more loving, and more trustworthy individuals.

In essence, I am saying that marriage is much more than a match of two people trying to achieve stability and security, although in the early years of marriage, they are a goal in and of themselves. But somewhere around the eighth to 12th year of marriage, the partners also start to want marital growth. Instead of marching the same road again and again, they long to see new territory and enjoy the scenery along the way. They want the opportunity to see how much they can offer as a couple.

It is important to remember that even though stability issues are the first developmental task in achieving marital "us-ness," security is next, and sincerity follows. They are always part of a marriage, but with different emphases at different times. For instance, a newly married couple is interested in security and how they can grow together, but it is stability that takes the greatest priority in the relationship, whereas spouses who have been married for five years are likely to make achieving security their priority. On the other hand, it is not unusual, for instance, to see spouses who have been married for 10 years or more who have not accomplished any sense of trustworthiness. Although it is certainly an issue for them, they will not be able to address sincerity because of the lack of stability and security in the relationship. It is those partners who have achieved a sense of stability and security who have the best chance of moving into a sincere and growing relational "us."

The research supports this idea that couples attain stability and security as a marriage progresses. Johnson (1985) reports that in older marriages, there are fewer fights over children, money, religion, and relatives. In other words, there is more security in the marriage. This idea of less conflict in older marriages is also supported by Levenson, Cartensen, and Gottman (1993).

But more compelling to me is the research into the types of marriages that develop over time. It tells me about a couple's quality of "us." Brubaker (1985) found that as partners stay married to each other, either their marriage improves slightly, it deteriorates slowly the more years they are married, or it stays about the same, whether the marriage is unhappy or happy. Similar findings have been revealed concerning couples who have either a stable positive, a stable negative, or a stable neutral relationship over the course of years (Weihaus & Field, 1988). These researchers found a small group that was curvilinear; that is, the marriage was good, but declined for a while, and then improved. However, in most cases, according to the research, the couple patterns tended to continue as they were (Ade-Ridder, 1985).

Lack of Sincerity

This research is meaningful because it indicates that if marriages do not achieve stability and security, they are generally unsatisfactory. But it also indicates that if a marriage is simply okay, that does not set the stage for a great marriage later on. Sincerity or growth in the marital relationship is necessary for the marriage to be the best it can.

Marriage offers a tremendous opportunity to become more satisfying and nurturing. It is indeed a shame when spouses simply go through the motions of what they learned together in the first 10 years of marriage for the decades after. They become so accustomed to how they do things together that they stop trying to nurture the relationship. As a result, the relational "us" becomes weak and begins to falter. Many such couples will stay married under these circumstances, but others will want something more out of the relationship, although they may find it difficult to say exactly what that is. In these situations, the lack of sincerity in the marriage produces two primary feelings: boredom and waning love.

Boredom

After marital partners have been together for a while but have not flourished, they look at the "us" and say, "Is this all there is?" People want to be emotionally satisfied and nurtured at deeper and deeper levels. When they find the marriage is stagnating, they turn away from the relational "us" and find other sources of nurture—work, infidelity, friendships, or hopeless complaining.

Work or Service

It is not unusual for spouses who are having marital difficulties to immerse themselves in work or civic or community service. Work or service gives them the chance to be productive, and to receive positive feedback. Work also can demand an enormous amount of time, so a bored spouse can give more and more of himself or herself to the job. Work or service also provides a bored partner with an excuse for not spending time at home.

Infidelity

As pointed out previously, all spouses are at potential risk for infidelity, but spouses who have not achieved sincerity are at special risk. Perhaps as many as 75% of men and 25% of women who divorce in the middle years of marriage have been unfaithful (Hayes, 1979). Dissatisfaction with the marriage prompts them to look elsewhere for excitement. Sexual or emotional infidelities are a sure cure for marital boredom, but they also destroy marital security and potential sincerity.

Friendships

There is certainly nothing wrong with spouses developing rich and rewarding friendships outside the marital "us-ness." But in some cases, these friendships substitute for the emotional nurturing and growth that should take place in a marriage. People who have difficulty with the issue of sincerity often are much closer to their friends than to their spouses. These friendships allow them to live the greater part of their married lives apart from each other, instead of as a couple.

Hopeless Complaining

Some spouses stay together, but handle the boredom in the relationship by complaining about how nothing ever happens and how they are stuck. In these situations, the complaining becomes a part of the relationship to the point that it is characteristic of the interactions between the spouses.

However, the complaining does not inspire either spouse to try to correct the problem. The hopeless complaining, therefore, causes no change in the relationship and allows the spouses to drift further apart.

Waning Love

Most partners who have made it to the second decade of marriage are trustworthy in terms of how they handle the marital work. However, for those who have not achieved sincerity, the lack of love is a common complaint. Although this lack of love usually is viewed as meaning a lack of romantic/erotic feeling, the complaint is more likely to refer to a lack of giving or companionship. Instead of wanting to give love and companionship to their partners, spouses frame their feelings in such a way that they do not feel loved. As a result of their perceiving a lack of love, they will often move toward selfishness, emotional separation, individual growth as opposed to couple growth, and midlife escapes from marriage.

Selfishness

Some spouses deal with this feeling of lack of love by exhibiting behavior that meets their own needs and does not encompass the needs of the marriage. The spouse infers that being denied the love to which he or she feels entitled justifies taking things from the marriage. Some spouses will spend household money on themselves because they "deserve it." Some will take vacation trips alone, while others will threaten to leave the relationship. This kind of destructive behavior puts the relational "us-ness" at risk and creates untrustworthy actions that can spiral the couple into instability and insecurity. Spouses seek to dominate each other instead of cooperating. Among couples who divorce in the middle years of marriage, only 17% of them had marriages in which they were equals (Hayes, 1979).

Emotional Separation

Spouses who do not feel loved by each other believe that trying to communicate is futile because the spouse does not care. Emotionally, the partners seal themselves off from each other and live separate lives. This behavior is what Gottman (1994) calls stonewalling. Among couples who divorce in the middle years of marriage, over 75% reported that there was *no communication* (Hayes, 1979).

Individual Growth Versus Couple Growth

Many couples may stay married legally, but function as though divorced, pursuing careers, friendships, and hobbies that exclude each other. It is not that they have stopped growing as individuals, they have simply stopped growing as a couple. Individual growth is fine and good, but when it is juxtaposed to couple growth, the marriage deteriorates.

Midlife Bolts from Marriage

Although there is significant evidence to debunk the idea of *midlife crisis* (Skolnick, 1987), the fact remains that many partners in the middle years of marriage leave the marriage for a new life. These "bolts" from the relationship may be a new career, new hobbies, a changed lifestyle, or a change in physical appearance, but at their base is a belief that the partner "deserves" something more than what the marital relationship offers.

When couples experience boredom and waning love, they will often come in for marital therapy, although some will seek therapy without a particular crisis occurring. In both cases, therapeutic work in the area of sincerity will enrich the couple's experience of "us-ness" and create a context for the development of a healthier relationship.

Key Attitudes for Sincerity

If spouses are going to explore the sincerity in their relationship and use the relationship as a context for self-growth, they must learn how to fight off the feelings of familiarity and boredom. In my experience with spouses who come in complaining of boredom and lack of love, there are two key attitudes that have not developed in the relational "us": *sacrifice* and *teachability*.

Sacrifice

I believe that there are two concepts that are helpful when thinking about the idea of sacrifice in marriage. The first is the idea of altruistic love, that is, to forfeit something that we really want or value for the sake of our spouse who wants or values something else. Think of the couple in the rowboat when one of the partners looks at the other and asks, "Where would you really like to go if you were the only one in the boat?" After the answer comes, the first partner says, "Well, I'm going to use my time and energy to help you get to that place." This is what is meant by sacrifice. One partner puts his or her own desires aside in order to help his or her spouse achieve the goals that the spouse desires.

Some examples of sacrifice in marriages are very complex and costly. For instance, a man left a successful business practice in the place where he had lived most of his life to move with his wife to a city were she had been offered a teaching position at a university. When asked why he would sacrifice so much of his own comfort, in terms of both lifestyle and finances, he responded as follows:

> There is some of this that I question. It will be hard for me to develop a new practice and we will suffer some financially. But I knew that teaching at a university has always been her dream. If she had not accepted this position, she would always look back at this time as her lost opportunity. In my mind, I had to make sure she had her opportunity. When faced with the alternative, the cost to me is not very high.

Some sacrifices may be smaller, but have just as dynamic an impact. I have seen people save for years in order to surprise a spouse with a particular gift. I have seen others put in hours of planning for parties or trips that the partner would enjoy. Thus, whether the sacrifice is large or small, the key factor is that one partner forfeits his or her own "right" in order to ensure that the other partner is able to get what he or she wants. In return, the sacrificing spouse usually feels intense joy as he or she sees his or her partner satisfied.

One of the questions that I am always asked when I talk about sacrifice is, "How can I be sure that my spouse won't take advantage of me?" The answer is, you cannot. Sacrifice by nature is giving without attention to self. That doesn't mean, however, that sacrifice in marriage is always justified. Sacrificial giving is appropriate in trustworthy relationships. It is inappropriate when one partner continually benefits by the sacrifice and never gives anything back. It is also inappropriate for the one who sacrifices to use it as a tool to try to force the partner into giving. But for those stable and secure relationships that have resulted in trust, sacrificial giving produces a sincere bond of the relational "us" and the giving becomes mutual.

The other concept that I find helpful when thinking about the practice of sacrifice in marriage comes from baseball. A sacrifice bunt is when the batter bunts the ball solely to get a base runner to the next base. Although most sacrifice bunters do not get to first base themselves, the bunt is seen as an effort to score runs for the good of the team.

In marriage, the relational "us" is the team. Some individual sacrifices are made not so much for the spouse as for the marriage. These sacrifices strengthen the quality of marriage. Also, these sacrifices usually include both spouses' giving. This was the case with a couple that had been married for 32 years and was having some difficulty over how to deal with an aging parent.

Husband: We have made some decisions regarding caring for Elizabeth's mother.

Therapist: What are they?

Husband: We have mutually decided that we will put her in a residential care facility during the week, but we will bring her to our home for the weekends.

Wife: My mother has always insisted that she not be put in a nursing home. We can't care for her during the week, but we can give her some comfort and honor her wishes part of the time.

Therapist: What changes will that bring for you two?

Husband: Many. For one, it will mean that my leisure activities will change radically. I will not be golfing every weekend and our social life will be curtailed.

Wife: We enjoy traveling together and were beginning to be able to travel more now that the kids have left. All of that will be delayed.

Therapist: Sounds like a lot of sacrifice for your mother.

Husband: That is true, but we both have this feeling that it is the right thing to do. We have always said that we want our marriage

to be one that people could point to as an example. We want
to do the right thing, not just the easy thing.

Therapist: So this is not just for your mother, but for your marriage?

Wife: I guess so. We have always been willing to do things for others and we are sort of known for doing that. Even though
there is pressure on us because of my mother, we want to do
this for her. It is in our nature.

Therapist: Is that good for the marriage?

Husband: It comes at a cost, but it is who we are. It is good for us and
we both feel better when we do these types of things.

In this situation, the couple is making individual sacrifices because of
the marital "us" quality of being giving and doing things for other people. The marital character is one of giving, so both partners are willing to
sacrifice in order for the marital giving to continue. These types of sacrifices, not only for individual growth but also for marital growth, result
in sincere bonding of the marital partners.

How then does sacrifice bring sincerity into a relationship and how
does it contribute to growth? First, it builds growth into the marital relationship by giving the spouses a sense of the things that they stand for as
an "us." The character of the "us" is seen as being worth the individual
sacrifices of the partners. Second, it builds individual growth as the
spouses sacrifice in order for the other to achieve goals and satisfy
desires. This makes the individual partners better and more successful
people. Finally, and most important, it contributes to individual growth
by allowing each spouse to learn how fulfilling it is to give to another.
The sacrifice may prevent me from reaching a personal goal, but it gives
me something much more precious. It gives me peace of mind by knowing that a person I love is happy and fulfilled.

Teachability

I heard Carl Whitaker say on many occasions to different groups,
"Nothing worth knowing can be taught, it must be learned." Being
teachable means that a person is willing to learn and change. Applied
to the marital relationship, it means that spouses are willing to use the

relationship as a means to learn about themselves so that they can make the changes appropriate to becoming better people.

All of us want to be accepted and loved for just being ourselves. This cuts to the core of who we are and makes us feel comfortable and loved. I am not suggesting that we give up the idea of acceptance of our spouse or of wanting to be accepted by our partner. Acceptance is part of love. What I am suggesting is that part of sincerity is that we start evaluating ourselves honestly in light of the fact that we are imperfect. Relationships are like a mirror. They show us who we are, how our behavior is perceived, and where we fit. We see a little of who we need to become, where our behavior is inappropriate, and how we must change to fit better in relationships, and this is especially true of the marital relationship.

In order to have a sincere relationship with my spouse, however, I cannot teach my spouse where he or she needs to change. Sincerity in the relationship means that I must learn *about myself*. I look at what the relationship reveals in me and then I seek to do the work on myself, not on my spouse. Alcoholics Anonymous puts it in terms of cleaning up your side of the fence. But it's difficult to look at our own issues honestly and sincerely and see where we need to change. It so difficult, in fact, that I find that couples often undermine the sincerity of their relationship by utilizing two techniques: *"I'll live with yours if you live with mine,"* and *"Yes, but...".*

I'll Live with Yours If You Live with Mine

Many times, spouses know which issues are problematic to their own personal growth and get in the way of the relationship. However, because their spouses also have issues that are problems, the couple comes to an agreement not to force the issue or require the other to change. In some instances, these agreements are overt, but most of the time they are covert until one of the spouses complains against the other. This can prompt bitter fighting as the spouses dredge up their frustration with each other. Such was the case with a couple that had been married for six years and had two children.

> Wife: It is difficult for me to talk about this, but it keeps getting to me more and more. Your table manners are really bad and besides bothering me, you're a bad example for the kids.

Husband: *(Instantly angry)* Yeah, right. You don't have anything wrong with you. What about your inability to get anything done around the house? You can't plan, you can't prioritize, you can't accomplish anything.

Wife: *(Very angry and crying)* I can't believe you would say that. What does that have to do with a simple issue of table manners. You know how sensitive that area is for me. If you want to start in on other issues, what about the pornography you keep in your dresser? You want to talk about that?

Husband: You're the one who started this. You say you want me to change, then we'll start talking about all the things that we need to change.

The couple had a covert agreement that they would tolerate each other's failings and problems. As long as they did not bring up each other's issues, they functioned in a stable relationship. However, each had serious work to do if the other was to feel connected and if the marital "us" relationship was to grow. The lack of teachability in the relationship resulted in an explosion when the woman broke the agreement by bringing up a problem.

Teachability is a willingness to face problems instead of trying to find comfort in denial or in the fact that the spouse has just as many problems or issues. Being teachable is, at least on some level, being enthusiastic about how the relationship can reveal an understanding of our shortcomings so that we can take steps to correct them and grow beyond them.

Yes, But...

This is related to the covert agreement between spouses to live with problems, but is different in that it is associated more with defensiveness than with denial. In using this technique, the partner will respond to each issue or problem brought up by the other with "Yes, but...." followed by some statement that is either an excuse, a logical defense of the action, or a counteraccusation.

In statements that are excuses, the spouse is intending to say, "I know what I do or who I am is a problem, but I have a sufficient reason to maintain the behavior." For instance, the following statement was made by a woman who was confronted about her raging at her husband and children with very little provocation.

I know that I shouldn't get so angry, but I came from a home where there was conflict and anger all the time. You know how we were physically and emotionally abused. I think I do pretty good to keep my temper as well as I do for one coming from my background.

When a spouse uses "Yes, but..." statements that are defended by logic, he or she is trying to create an elaborate intellectual means to maintain behavior that he or she does not want to change. In one such situation with a couple in therapy, the husband was extremely controlling and would not allow his wife to use any money from their bank account. Instead, he would stingily dole out cash for his wife to spend. When confronted with his control problems, he defended his actions by explaining that he kept all the financial records on his computer and that it was essential that they be correct. He explained that if he did not handle the finances in this way, the record keeping would be compromised and it would be impossible to pay the bills on time or report their taxes correctly.

Finally, when a spouse voices counteraccusations, the intent of the accusations is to throw the partner off balance. In other words, if I can get my spouse to focus on his or her problem, or at least instigate an argument over the interaction, I can deflect the issue. These counteraccusations very often do redirect the couple's attention to another issue, and may result in conflict.

The problem with "Yes, but..." statements is that they are defensive responses that keep the spouse from dealing with what most needs to change. It is important to remember that whereas not everything that spouses say about each other is true, their accusations usually do have an element of truth. Teachability means that the spouse is willing to listen to what the relationship tells him or her. It means listening to the good and bad, and then honestly sorting through the bad to find what is true without excusing it, defending it with logic, or deflecting it through counteraccusation. Everyone has things they need to change about themselves. Teachability is the willingness to make those changes.

Making Sincerity Work in the Relational "Us"

When a couple comes to therapy with sincerity as the primary issue, it is essential than to help the spouses focus on the relational "us." There is sacrifice for the good of a partner, but most of the reason for sacrifice and being teachable is to enhance the quality of the marital "us-ness." It is not just compromise; it is finding out what goals and behaviors fit the relationship. Sometimes that will be the goals and behaviors that one spouse wants, sometimes it will be those of the other, and sometimes it will be an amalgamation of the two.

In my clinical practice, I find that sincerity is not the result of a correction in the marriage as are stability and security. Sincerity either happens or it doesn't. In other words, some spouses negotiate sincerity naturally. They make sacrifices and are teachable as a normal part of the marriage. Those who don't have sincerity usually have no idea of how to put sacrifice and teachability into practice. Most times, I make assignments to help these couples work out and practice the sincerity issues.

Goals and Dreams

If the spouses are going to make sincere moves toward "us" in terms of sacrifice, they must know each other's goals and dreams, although most marriage partners do not regularly communicate about their aspirations. The communication of goals and dreams can benefit a couple in several ways. First, it puts the spouses in a position to communicate outside the daily routine. This gives them time to think about what is really important to them and to consider what they want their marriage to stand for. This is part of getting in touch with the "soul" of the marriage. Second, communicating about goals and dreams provides direction. Couples do not have good or bad marriages intentionally, but just stumble into the ditch or on the highway without paying much attention. To paraphrase the Chinese proverb, "If a couple has a target to shoot for, they are more likely to hit it." Third, communicating goals and dreams forces the spouses to consider the possibility of sacrifice to find out whether or not the goal or dream is possible. Even if they later decide that the goal is not attainable, considering the possibility of and willingness to sacrifice makes other sacrifices more likely. Finally, talking about goals and dreams gets the "us" moving. In my practice, it is extremely rare to find spouses who will talk about goals and dreams without taking some action. Consider part of the therapy session with a couple who had been married for 10 years and had two children. They had come in because of their general dissatisfaction with the marriage and the belief that they were beginning to fight more and more.

Therapist: *(To the wife)* What goals do you have for yourself or your marriage?

Wife: *(Pause)* I'm not sure about the marriage, but I have always had a goal for myself...I hesitate to even say it out loud.

Husband: Go ahead and say it.

Wife: I have wanted to study physical therapy. You knew I wanted to do that before we married.

Husband: *(Pause)* You have never brought it up since we married. I thought that you wanted to be a stay-at-home mom and you haven't said anything else.

Wife: I did want to be a stay-at-home mom, but now that the kids are both starting school, I have thought about this more.

There was no physical therapy school in their area, so the woman considered it an impossibility. The husband, although surprised by his wife's goal, was interested even though he did not see any possibilities either. However, when the couple came back to therapy the next week, there were some surprising developments.

Wife: We left here last week and Joe got on the Internet.

Husband: On the way home, I started thinking about this airline commercial I saw where a woman was commuting to law school each week by plane. So I started exploring the possibilities.

Wife: He found a school where I could finish most of my undergraduate classes by taking one night class a week and another on the weekend. Then he found another school that specializes in offering physical-therapy programs designed for commuters.

Husband: We will have to do some figuring to enable her to do clinical work, but if we get her through the course requirements, then I think we will find a way for her to finish.

Therapist: That is a big change from being impossible.

Husband: It has really given me something to focus on and has really energized me. I never knew she wanted to go in that direction.

Wife: I can't tell you what this has done for me. It is like someone came out and threw me a lifeline.

Often, as here, spouses will be willing to make sacrifices for each other if they know what the other wants. In cases where the couple will not work together or one spouse does not want to allow the other to make a sacrifice for him or her, the therapist can explore the reason in depth and help them to confront the patterns or beliefs that are making the giving or accepting of sacrifice difficult. But many times, couples will respond to the type of goal and dream exploration found in the next exercise.

❧ *Couple Exercise Thirteen*

Goals and Dreams

Many times, spouses are willing to make sacrifices for each other and the relationship, but are unaware of what the goals and dreams of their partners are about. This exercise is intended to help you identify what goals and dreams you would like to attain.

Individual Goals and Dreams
1. List some personal goals or dreams that you have for yourself individually. Try to place these according to priority.
2. Identify some of the reasons why you have been unable to accomplish these goals or dreams.
3. Look at your spouse's answers for #1 and #2. Are there any sacrifices that you could make that would remove the barriers to his or her being able to attain the goal or dream? Identify these and state your willingness or unwillingness to take these actions.
4. Decide together whether any of the goals and dreams on the list are doable.

Couple Goals and Dreams
1. What are some of the goals and dreams you have as a couple or a relational "us"? State these according to a priority.
2. Identify some of the barriers to these goals and dreams.
3. How might both of you sacrifice and work together to make some of these goals and dreams a reality? State your willingness or unwillingness to take these actions.

Good Sex

Sex is a good topic of discussion when it comes to sincerity because it requires both sacrifice and teachability. It is important to point out here that I am not suggesting that all sexual problems are a result of insincerity. Many sexual issues with couples are physiologically based and any therapist who is helping a couple with these problems should thoroughly explore that possibility. However, many sexual problems also are a result of lack of education and communication, a lack of familiarity, or an unwillingness to change.

Education and Communication

One of the big hurdles that we face in Western society is how people get information concerning sex and sexuality and how it translates into belief systems. We are sexually schizophrenic, by which I mean that we are confused about reality. We are bombarded by religion, government, and parents with essentially the same conservative message: just don't do it. At the same time, we are also inundated with the liberal message that sex feels good and will be so fulfilling that even your neighbor will have to have a cigarette. As a result, society is neither pro- nor antisexual. It is both. I find this schizophrenic attitude among my students in conservative Amarillo, Texas. When I ask, most of them will profess being for premarital sex (a liberal idea) and against extramarital sex (a conservative idea). They will be for abortion rights but against gay rights. They will advocate more sexual freedom and less sex education. If that sounds crazy, it is. But the fact is that we all probably harbor some of those same contradictions. What we need, of course, is clarity and balance, and so in therapy, I try to help a couple identify some of their more extreme beliefs about sex and move them toward a more balanced and reasonable view.

One of the most difficult issues for couples who grow up in a schizophrenic society is communication about sex. Although we are constantly exposed to sexually explicit messages, we feel that we should not talk about sex and sexual performance during sexual acts. I do not find it unusual for spouses to be unable to use sexual language to describe bodily parts to their partners and certainly I find that they have much difficulty in expressing what they like and dislike, what feels good and what hurts. Part of moving the couple toward balance is confronting these ideas about sexuality and helping them to learn how to communicate with each other.

Lack of Familiarity

In a society in which we receive such confusing information about sex, it is little wonder that couples are unfamiliar with the idea of sacrifice for the sake of satisfaction. Basically, this means giving in order to get, as I described in Chapter 1 in relation to the elements of "us-ness."

If there is any act that illustrates "us-ness" better than sex, then I am not aware of it. Most spouses bring into the marriage the idea that their sexual satisfaction is their own business and responsibility. They have been trained to believe that if they are unable to reach orgasm, then there is something wrong with them; that is, they concentrate on themselves, not on their partners. I have found it helpful for spouses to focus on satisfying the other, for a couple of reasons. First, for the majority of couples, doing what satisfies the partner will take off the pressure and allow the spouse to proceed by doing what comes naturally. Second, when both partners are engaged in looking out for what will satisfy the other, there is mutual sacrifice, and usually both are satisfied. This does not mean that partners should not direct each other to what feels pleasurable. Couples must communicate before, during, and after sex. They are doing each other a favor by letting the other know what is working and what feels good.

When spouses engage in this type of sacrificing, concentrating on each other's satisfaction, and communicating with each other, the couple starts to develop an "us" sexual identity. In other words, the partners develop ways in which the sexual relationship will work best for both, instead of just accommodating one of them or alternating pleasuring activities. This familiarity with the "us" sexual relationship enables comfort and reliability.

Unwillingness to Change

Some spouses are unwilling to be teachable about sex, perhaps because they are unwilling to change a fundamental belief or refocus from their own satisfaction to that of the partner. Or it may be that they consider some sexual act "wrong" or "perverted," or that their egos are too fragile to allow them to follow directions. Whatever the reason, the inability to change sexual habits can be so deeply ingrained, possibly as a result of societal, family-of-origin, or personal experiences, that even the most powerful of logic does not induce change. No matter how good the information or how skilled the therapist, sometimes reasoning does not change behavior.

In these instances, it is possible to have the couple work toward sexual sincerity, even though there are going to be specified limits of giving and sacrifice. Couples are able to enjoy sex even while focusing more on the companionship and security of the relationship (Reedy, Birren, & Schaie, 1982). One couple, married 17 years, enjoyed a satisfying relationship in many areas, but were in conflict over an unsatisfactory sex life. Both spouses had done substantial work in rooting out some of their problematic belief patterns and had begun to develop a good sense of "us" in the sexual relationship. However, they had problems with coming to an agreement on all sexual activity.

Husband: Things are much better. I feel we are moving toward a good sexual relationship, but it is still not there.

Therapist: What is holding you back?

Husband: I would like us to be freer to try new things in our sexual relationship. There are some things that I enjoy that she doesn't.

Wife: He's talking about oral sex. He likes it and I don't.

Therapist: Have you talked about it?

Wife: We've discussed it many times. When he does it to me, it is enjoyable. But I just can't do it for him. I mean, I know there is nothing wrong with it, but I still haven't been able to get over it. It is just a shutdown for me.

Therapist: How does that work out for you *(to the husband)*?

Husband: It depends. There are times where I am okay with it and think that if the sex is better, I don't have to try new things. But there are other times where I think that I have a right to want her to please me. I kind of get trapped in feeling like she should do it because I like it—because it is something that she can do to sacrifice for me.

Wife: And that is part of the shutdown for me. I feel as though I should be willing to please him, but when I feel myself shut down, I am not able to. That just brings on the guilt.

Therapist: And what have you tried so far?

Wife: We've tried to communicate openly about it. We get through sex, but it is more difficult.

Husband: I know that if I bring it up during sex, we will have difficulty.

Therapist: There are difficult issues like this that are not so easy to resolve. One of you wants something from the other, but giving it brings dissatisfaction to the other. It is probably going to be unrealistic to think that we can solve every problem at once, so we probably need to set some parameters that allow you to proceed with your sexual life without getting hung up here. Tell me *(to the husband)*, are there areas where she is changing and focusing on giving you pleasure?

Husband: Yes. She has been willing to take more time to concentrate on sex and to be more aggressive.

Therapist: *(To the wife)* Has this worked for you?

Wife: Yes, it has been very good for both of us.

Therapist: If this issue of oral sex were not brought up during sex, would you continue to do some communicating about the issue and thinking about it at other times.

Wife: When we are not having sex? Yes, that would relieve a lot of pressure.

Therapist: If she continued to work on the issue, could you focus on the things in which you both are successful in sex and not bring up oral sex except at times when you are not having sex?

Husband: If I knew she would at least keep thinking about it, that would be enough for me. Like I said, things are getting much better.

In the sexual relationship, as in the whole of life, the spouses are not going to be perfectly sacrificial and teachable in every area. The focus of therapy with spouses who are facing sexual issues is to keep them heading in the right direction of sacrificing and being teachable. I utilize the following couple exercise to help them identify some of their difficulties in their sexual relationship.

❧ *Couple Exercise Fourteen*

Improving Giving and Change in the Sexual Relationship

In order to have a sincere sexual relationship, it is necessary to focus on giving and satisfying your partner (sacrifice) and being willing to change or modify your own sexual ideas or practices (being teachable). The following questions are intended to give you an idea of how to go about this change.

Conservative Ideas

Many of our sexual ideas are influenced by traditionally conservative institutions that are interested in limiting sexual pleasure to marriage or to ensure that sex is used only for procreation. Among these are parents, religious institutions, governments, and schools. How have these institutions influenced your ideas about what is "right" and "wrong" about sex?

Liberal Ideas

Many of our sexual ideas also are influenced by traditionally liberal institutions that are interested in exploiting sexual pleasure for happiness or using it in media campaigns. Among these are our peers, movies and television, the music industry, and the advertising media. How have these institutions influenced your ideas about what is "good" or is "bad" sex?

1. Most people have both conservative and liberal ideas about sex, which may contribute to their confusion. How can you move toward a more balanced view of sex instead of being influenced by your past?
2. Are you and your spouse able to communicate about sex in accurate terms? What can you do to be more comfortable with talking about sex?
3. Are you and your spouse able to talk about what pleases you both? If not, what are some reasons that you find it difficult to communicate? How can you change this pattern?
4. What are some areas of sexual pleasure that you would like to have in your sexual relationship?
5. How might you imagine your spouse's providing this pleasure?
6. Look at your partner's answers to #4 and #5. What would you be willing to do to make you partner more satisfied sexually?
7. What are some areas where it would be difficult for you to bring him or her pleasure? Why?
8. How can you continue to work on these areas so that your spouse will know that you are continuing to consider change?

Personal Growth

I am all for people pursuing their personal goals and ambitions, and am particularly interested in seeing their spouses sacrifice to make those goals a reality. However, the personal growth that I am talking about here is not about what a spouse can sacrifice to help a partner, but what the partner can learn from the relationship in order to become a better person.

Again, relationships are mirrors that show us our strengths and weaknesses, our good and bad points. When we consider personal growth from this angle, we are asking spouses to look into the relational mirror, and when they see their weaknesses or bad points, we ask them to have the teachability to change. As therapists, we do this by helping the spouses recognize that when they have a particular unpleasant or angry feeling, it may indicate something that they need to change. The natural reaction to these types of feelings is to blame them on the spouse: "If only he or she would do something different or be something different, I wouldn't feel this way." But this reaction does not help the spouses to learn about themselves. For example, the following is from a session with a couple that had been married for 19 years. They had two adolescent sons and the wife was very dissatisfied with the husband's performance as a father.

Wife: You *(to her husband)* are not there enough for the boys. I would think that you would be attending weekend programs that could help you learn to be a better father and husband. I think that you would want the best relationship with them and me that you could have.

Husband: I do want a good relationship. I just don't go about it in the way you want me to.

Therapist: Margie, what is it you want?

Wife: I want him to be a better father and husband.

Therapist: And what would that look like?

Wife: *(Pauses and then laughs)* It would look like the way I want it.

Therapist: I think so. So what does your feeling about the way your husband goes about parenting and loving you tell you about you?

Wife: What does my frustration tell me about me?

Therapist: Yes.

Wife: *(Long pause)* It tells me that I am a controlling bitch.

Therapist: I don't think you are a controlling bitch, but I do that think it tells you that you have an issue with wanting people to do things your way. I can work on the issue of your husband with him, but how can I help you work on this overmanaging that results in so much frustration?

Working toward personal growth does not only mean working toward personal goals and plans. It is learning how to look at the marital relationship and my reactions in that relationship in order to learn about myself. Some reactions are not pleasant, and certainly are not justified. Being teachable means that I will have the courage to look squarely at those unpleasant things and then go about the tough work of changing them.

❧ *Couple Exercise Fifteen*

Using the Relationship to Grow

We often will find ourselves angry or frustrated with our spouses, children, or friends. Our tendency then is to blame our frustration or anger on the behavior, being, or reactions of the other person. People are imperfect, and sometimes they do need to change. However, many times, our anger or frustration points out something that we need to change about ourselves.

For instance, there was a father who was convinced that his children were too disobedient and unreliable. He was always criticizing their behavior. He also considered his wife too oriented toward the children and would often get angry because he thought she was too nurturing. True, his children did misbehave and his wife was too "soft" at times, but his feelings also pointed out some flaws in himself. He conceded that he was too hard because he always wanted things to go his way so that he would not be disturbed. He was so rigid because basically he did not want to be bothered.

When we become frustrated or angry in our marriage, it is a good practice to look at what those feelings say about us. Being teachable means that we make an honest appraisal of ourselves and start taking actions to change.

1. Think about the last time you were angry or frustrated with your spouse. What were some of the things that were troubling you?
2. Whether or not your anger or frustration was justified, what do those feelings in that situation point to in you that may need to change?
3. What are some ways in which you might go about changing this behavior or belief?

❧ ❧ ❧

202 THE ESSENTIAL HUMILITY OF MARRIAGE

Building a Legacy

Think about your great-grandparents. If you are like most people, you do not even know the full names of those eight people who provided your genetic heritage. Yet, even though you might not be aware of who they are, you undoubtedly look, think, and act more like them than like any of your contemporaries. Now ask yourself: In just three generations, will my descendants not even be aware that I have lived? As for me personally, I travel and lecture. I do therapy weekly trying to help people to solve life's problems. I write professional articles and books. But when I am gone, the books will be out of print and my accomplishments will soon be forgotten. What can I do so that I will live on in the memories of my great-grandchildren?

Many of the couples with whom we deal in therapy are so trapped in the "here-and-now" framework that they forget that they are building a legacy for their children, friends, and community. When they are gone, people will not remember their accomplishments or financial success, but they will remember the quality of the couple's "us-ness." This is the example that they will set on how to live in relationships and, at a minimum, will model a balanced sense of life.

In introducing the idea of legacy to a couple, the therapist is once again introducing a powerful approach to help the spouses think outside themselves. Most, when they consider what they will leave to posterity, will think in terms of enduring values—in essence, loving well and being trustworthy. Helping the spouses concentrate on their legacy will give them relational direction. This was the case with spouses who were having difficulty with what they called constant "bickering." The current "bickering" was about the husband's committing to do a favor for a friend.

Wife: You give too much to other people. They take advantage of you.

Husband: Why should that bother you? It is not hurting you.

Therapist: *(Stopping the quarrel)* You know, I just had this thought about what you two stand for in your relationship. Both of you are obviously good people, but together, you always seem to be fighting.

Wife: That's for sure.

Therapist: I wonder what people will say about you two when you are gone.

Husband: Probably just what you said. Individually they were pretty good folks, but they never could get along together.

Wife: *(More contemplative)* I hadn't thought of it in that way. We don't look good. We wouldn't be remembered well.

Therapist: How would you like to be remembered as a couple?

Wife: *(Pause)* I guess more like we would be remembered individually. That we're giving to folks and we're happy.

Therapist: How about you *(to the husband)*?

Husband: *(More seriously)* Yeah. I would like us to be remembered as helpful and happy.

Therapist: Then how can both of you learn to fit with one another better so that you can be remembered well?

In this case, as in most, when the issue of legacy is introduced, the spouses stop the current argument and become more introspective. As a result of introspection, they will usually take their behavior and action more seriously. It is as if they suddenly realize that they only have a limited time to make an impact together. They begin to consider what the legacy of their relational "us" will be.

✧ *Couple Exercise Sixteen*

What Will Your Legacy Be?

1. Consider for a few moments the possibility of being present at your own funerals. Say the two of you were buried side by side with one headstone. What would be a fitting epitaph that would describe how people would remember your relationship?
2. How would you like them to remember your relationship?
3. What benefits would your children, friends, and the community get from your relationship if you could be remembered in this positive way?

4. What changes would you need to make in order for the description to become a reality?

Conclusions

Sincerity is learning how to utilize a relationship to make headway toward growth, both as a couple and as individuals. The two key elements in making this journey of sincerity are sacrifice and teachability. These two attitudes can be applied in a variety of ways to assist the couple in identifying a closer and stronger "us" relationship. Sincerity is like the crown of the marital "us-ness." Stability tells the partners that they can be safe and live together. Security tells them that they can do the work of marriage in a trustworthy way and get things accomplished. But sincerity tells the spouses that they can be, individually and together, fulfilled and contributing. Sincerity cannot happen without stability and security, but it completes the marital relationship and puts the couple in touch with the soul of "us-ness."

References

Ade-Ridder, L. (1985). Quality of marriage: A comparison between golden wedding couples and couples married less than fifty years. *Lifestyles: A Journal of Changing Patterns, 7*, 224–237.

Ainsworth, M.D.S. (1989). Attachments beyond infancy. *American Psychologist, 44*, 709–716.

Albrecht, S.L. (1979). Correlates of marital happiness among the remarried. *Journal of Marriage and the Family, 41*, 862.

Albrecht, S.L., Bahr, H.M., & Goodman, K. (1983). *Divorce and remarriage: Problems, adaptations, and adjustments.* Westport, CT: Greenwood Press.

Amato, P.R., & Booth, A. (1997). *A generation at risk: Growing up in an era of family upheaval.* Cambridge, MA: Harvard University Press.

Arond, M., & Pauker, S.L. (1987). *The first year of marriage.* New York: Warner Books.

Baucom, D.H., & Hoffman, J.A. (1986). The effectiveness of marital therapy: Current status and application to the clinical setting. In N.S. Jacobson & A.S. Gurman (Eds.), *Clinical handbook of marital therapy* (pp. 597–620). New York: Guilford.

Baumrind, D. (1991). The influence of parenting style on adolescent competence and substance abuse. *Journal of Early Adolescence, 11,* 56–95.

Blair, S.L. (1993). Employment, family, and perceptions of marital quality among husbands and wives. *Journal of Family Issues, 14,* 189–212.

Book, C.L. (1980). *Human communication: Principles, contexts, and skills.* New York: St. Martin's Press.

Boszormenyi-Nagy, I., & Krasner, B. (1980). Trust-based therapy: A contextual approach. *American Journal of Psychiatry, 137,* 767–775.

Boszormenyi-Nagy, I., & Krasner, B. (1986). *Between give and take.* New York: Brunner/Mazel.

Bowen, M. (1978). *Family therapy in clinical practice.* New York: Jason Aronson.

Brubaker, T.H. (1985). *Later life families.* Beverly Hills, CA: Sage.

Buber, M. (1958). *I and thou.* New York: Scribner.

Crohan, S.E. (1992). Marital quality and conflict across the transition to parenthood in African American and white couples. *Journal of Marriage and the Family, 58,* 933–944.

Doherty, W.J. (1992). Private lives, public values. *Psychology Today, 25,* 32–37.

Doherty, W.J. (1996). *Soul searching: Why psychotherapy must promote moral responsibility.* New York: Basic Books.

Dreikurs, R., & Soltz, V. (1964). *Children: The challenge.* New York: Hawthorne Books.

Dunn, R.L., & Schwebel, A.I. (1995). Meta-analytic review of marital therapy outcome research. *Journal of Family Psychology. 9,* 58–68.

Exter, T.G. (1991). Birthrate debate. *American Demographics, 13,* 55.

Fathalla, M. (1992). Reproductive health: A key to a brighter future. Report from the World Health Organization, June 24, Geneva.

Fowers, B.J., Montel, K.H., & Olson, D.H. (1996). Predicting marital success for premarital couple types based on PREPARE. *Journal of Marital and Family Therapy*, 22(1), 103–119.

Fowers, B.J., & Olson, D.H. (1993). Five types of marriage: Empirical typology based on ENRICH. *The Family Journal: Counseling and Therapy for Couples and Families*, 1(3), 196–207.

Friedlander, M.L., Wildman, J., Heatherington, L., & Skowron, E.A. (1994). What we do and don't know about the process of family therapy. *Journal of Family Psychology*, 7, 57–75.

Fuchs, V.R. (1988). *Women's quest for economic equality*. Cambridge, MA: Harvard University Press.

Gallup, G. (1989). *Love and marriage*. Princeton, NJ: Gallup Organization.

Gelles, R.J., & Cornell, C.P. (1987). *Intimate violence in families* (2nd ed.). Newbury Park, CA: Sage.

Glass, S., & Wright, T. (1992). Justifications for extramarital relationships: The association between attitudes, behaviors and gender. *Journal of Sex Research*, 29, 361–387.

Glick, P. (1989). Remarried families, stepfamilies, and stepchildren: A brief demographic analysis. *Family Relations*, 48, 24–27.

Gordon, L.H. (1990). *Love knots*. New York: Dell.

Gottman, J. (1991). Predicting the longitudinal course of marriages. *Journal of Marital and Family Therapy*, 17, 3–7.

Gottman, J. (1994). *Why marriages succeed or fail and how you can make yours last*. New York: Fireside.

Gottman, J., & Gottman, J. (1998). *Out of the love lab: The marriage survival kit*. Speech given at the Second Annual Conference of the Coalition for Marriage, Family and Couples Education, Washington, D.C., July 8–12.

Gough, K.E. (1971). The origins of the family. *Journal of Marriage and the Family, 33*, 760–771.

Grunebaum, H. (1997). Thinking about romantic/erotic love. *Journal of Marital and Family Therapy, 23*(3), 295–307.

Guadagno, M.A.N. (1983). Economic stress: Family financial managment. In C.R. Figley & H.I. McCubbin (Eds.), *Stress and the family: Coping with normative transitions (Vol. I)* (pp. 201–217). New York: Brunner/Mazel.

Guerin, P.J., Fay, L.F., Burden, S.L., & Kautto, J.G. (1987). *The evaluation and treatment of marital conflict*. New York: Basic Books.

Hahlweg, K., & Markman, H.J. (1988). Effectiveness of behavioral marital therapy: Empirical status of behavioral techniques in preventing and alleviating marital distress. *Journal of Consulting and Clinical Psychology, 56*, 440–447.

Hargrave, T.D. (1994). *Families and forgiveness: Healing wounds in the intergenerational family*. New York: Brunner/Mazel.

Hargrave, T.D. (in press). *Forgiving the devil*. Phoenix, AZ: Zeig, Tucker & Co.

Hargrave, T.D., & Anderson, W.T. (1992). *Finishing well: Aging and reparation in the intergenerational family*. New York: Brunner/Mazel.

Hargrave, T.D., & Sells, J.N. (1997). The development of a forgiveness scale. *Journal of Marital and Family Therapy, 23*, 41–62.

Hayes, M.P. (1979). Strengthening marriage in the middle years. In N. Stinnett, B. Chesser, & J. DeFrain (Eds.), *Building family strengths: Blueprints for action* (pp. 387–398). Lincoln, NB: University of Nebraska Press.

Hendrix, H. (1988). *Getting the love you want: A guide for couples*. New York: HarperCollins.

Hite, S. (1989). *The Hite report.* New York: Dell.

Hochschild, A. (1989). *The second shift: Working parents and the revolution at home.* New York: Viking Penguin.

Humphrey, F. (1987). Treating extramarital sexual relationships in sex and couples therapy. In G.Weeks & L. Hof (Eds.), *Integrating sex and marital therapy: A clinical guide* (pp. 149–170). New York: Brunner/Mazel.

Jacobson, N.S., & Addis, M.E. (1993). Research on couples and couple therapy: What do we know? Where are we going? *Journal of Consulting and Clinical Psychology, 61,* 85–93.

Jacobson, N.S., & Gottman, J. (1998). *When men batter women: New insights into ending abusive relationships.* New York: Simon & Schuster.

Jacobson, N.S., & Margolin, G. (1979). *Marital therapy: Strategies based on social learning and behavior exchange principles.* New York: Brunner/Mazel.

Jacobson, N.S., Schmaling, K.B., & Holtzworth-Munroe, A. (1987). Component analysis of behavioral marital therapy: Two-year follow-up and prediction of relapse. *Journal of Marital and Family Therapy, 13,* 187–195.

Johnson, C.L. (1985). The impact of illness on late-life marriages. *Journal of Marriage and the Family, 47,* 165–172.

Kieffer, C. (1977). New depths in intimacy. In R.W. Libby & R.N. Whitehurst (Eds.), *Marriage and alternatives: Exploring intimate relationships* (pp. 267-293). Glenview, IL: Scott, Foresman.

Kilmann, R., & Thomas, K. (1975). Interpersonal conflict: Handling behavior as reflections of Jungian personality dimensions. *Psychological Reports, 37,* 971–980.

Kinsey, A.C., Pomeroy, W.B., Martin, C.E., & Gebhard, P.H. (1953). *Sexual behavior in the human female.* Philadelphia: Saunders.

Levenson, R.W., Carstensen, L.L., & Gottman, J.M. (1993). Long-term marriage: Age, gender, and satisfaction. *Psychology and Aging, 8*, 301–313.

Lusterman, D. D. (1995). Treating marital infidelity. In R.H. Mikesell, D.D. Lusterman, & S.H. McDaniel (Eds.), *Integrating family therapy: Handbook of family psychology and systems theory* (pp. 259–269). Washington, DC: American Psychological Association.

Mace, D., & Mace, V. (1979). Enriching marriage. In N. Stinnet (Ed.), *Family strengths*. Lincoln, NB: University of Nebraska Press.

Margolis, M. (1984). *Mothers and such: Views of American women and why they changed*. Berkeley, CA: University of California Press.

Markman, H.J., Renick, M.J., Floyd, F.J., Stanley, S.M., & Clements, M. (1993). Preventing marital distress through communication and conflict management training: A 4 and 5 year follow-up. *Journal of Consulting and Clinical Psychology, 61*, 70–77.

Markman, H.J., Stanley, S., & Blumberg, S.L. (1994). *Fighting for your marriage: Positive steps for preventing divorce and preserving a lasting love*. San Francisco: Jossey-Bass.

Maslow, A.H. (1971). *The farther reaches of human nature*. New York: Viking.

McGoldrick, M., & Gerson, R. (1985). *Genograms in family assessment*. New York: Norton.

Miller, B.C., & Myers-Walls, J.A. (1983). Parenthood: Stresses and coping strategies. In C.R. Figley & H.I. McCubbin (Eds.), *Stress and the family: Coping with normative transitions (Vol. I)* (pp. 54–73). New York: Brunner/Mazel.

Minuchin, S., & Fishman, H.C. (1981). *Family therapy techniques*. Cambridge, MA: Harvard University Press.

Ney, P.G. (1992). Transgenerational abuse. In E.C. Viano (Ed.), *Intimate violence: Interdisciplinary perspectives*. Washington, DC: Hemisphere.

O'Leary, D.K. (1993). Through a psychological lens: Personality traits, personality disorders, and levels of violence. In R. Gelles & D. Loseke (Eds.), *Current controversies in family violence*. Newbury Park, CA: Sage.

Olson, D.H., & DeFrain, J. (1997). *Marriage and the family: Diversity and strengths* (2nd ed.). Mountain View, CA: Mayfield.

Olson, D.H., Fournier, D.G., & Druckman, J.M. (1989). *PREPARE, PREPARE-MC, and ENRICH inventories* (3rd ed.). Minneapolis: PREPARE/ENRICH.

Perlman, D., & Duck, S. (1987). *Intimate relationships*. Newbury Park, CA: Sage.

Poduska, B.E. (1993). *For love and money: A guide to finances and relationships*. Pacific Grove, CA: Brooks/Cole.

Reedy, M.N., Birren, J.E., & Schaie, K.W. (1982). Age and sex differences in satisfying love relationships across the adult life span. *Human Development, 24,* 52–66.

Renick, M.J., Blumberg, S.L., & Markman, H.J. (1992). The prevention and relationship enhancement program (PREP): An empirically based prevention intervention program for couples. *Family Relations, 41,* 992–1002.

Rogers, C.R. (1961). *On becoming a person: A therapist's view of psychotherapy*. Boston: Houghton Mifflin.

Rubin, L.B. (1985). *Just friends: The role of friendship in our lives*. New York: Harper & Row.

Rueter, M.A., & Conger, R.D. (1995). Antecedents of parent-adolescent disagreements. *Journal of Marriage and the Family, 57,* 435–448.

Satir, V. (1988). *The new peoplemaking* (rev. ed.). Mountain View, CA: Science & Behavior Books.

Saxton, L. (1993). *The individual, marriage, and the family* (8th ed.). Belmont, CA: Wadsworth.

Schaninger, C.M., & Buss, W.C. (1986). A longitudinal comparison of consumption and finance handling between happily married and divorced couples. *Journal of Marriage and the Family, 48,* 129–136.

Skolnick, A.S. (1987). *The intimate environment: Exploring marriage and the family* (4th ed.). Boston: Little Brown.

Smith, T. (1993). *American sexual behavior: Trends, socio-demographic differences, and risk behavior.* Chicago: National Opinion Research Center, University of Chicago.

Snyder, D.K., Willis, R.M., & Grady-Fletcher, A. (1991). Long-term effectiveness of behavioral versus insight-oriented marital therapy: A 4-year follow-up study. *Journal of Consulting and Clinical Psychology, 59,* 138–141.

Sperry, L., & Carlson, J. (1991). *Marital therapy: Integrating theory and technique.* Denver, CO: Love Publishing.

Stosny, S. (1998). *Compassion workshops.* Workshop given at the Second Annual Conference of the Coalition for Marriage, Family and Couples Education, Washington, D.C., July 8–12.

Tannen, D. (1990). *You just don't understand: Women and men in conversation.* New York: Ballantine Books.

Thoits, P.A. (1992). Identity structures and psychological well-being: Gender and marital status comparisons. *Social Psychology Quarterly, 55,* 236–256.

U.S. Bureau of the Census. (1994). *Statistical abstract of the United States* (114th ed.). Washington, DC: U.S. Government Printing Office.

U.S. Bureau of the Census. (1995). *Statistical abstract of the United States* (115th ed.). Washington, DC: U.S. Government Printing Office.

Voydanoff, P. (1991). Economic distress and family relations: A review of the eighties. In A. Booth (Ed.), *Contemporary families: Looking forward, looking back* (pp. 429–445). Minneapolis: National Council on Family Relations.

Walker, L. (1979). *The battered woman syndrome.* New York: Harper.

Weishaus, S., & Field, D. (1988). A half century of marriage: Continuity or change? *Journal of Marriage and the Family, 50*, 763–774.

Whitehead, B.D. (1996). *The divorce culture: Rethinking our commitments to marriage and family*. New York: Vintage Books.

Yllo, K. (1993). Through a feminist lens: Gender, power, and violence. In R. Gelles & D. Loseke (Eds.), *Current controversies in family violence*. Newbury Park, CA: Sage.

Index